Moving *into a* New Now

Other Books by Mildred Tengbom:

Is Your God Big Enough?

The Bonus Years (revised as *September Morning*)

Table Prayers

A Life to Cherish (reissued as *Devotions for New Mothers*)

Especially for Mother

No Greater Love: The Story of Clara Maass

Mealtime Prayers

Does Anyone Care How I Feel?

I Wish I Felt Good All the Time

Does It Make Any Difference What I Do?

Talking Together about Love and Sexuality

Sometimes I Hurt

Help for Bereaved Parents

Help for Families of the Terminally Ill

Bible Readings for Mothers

Sing to the Lord

The Spirit of God Was Moving

Grief for a Season

Coauthored with Luverne C. Tengbom:

Bible Readings for Families

Fill My Cup, Lord

Moving *into a* New Now

Faith *for the* Later Years

FROM THE JOURNALS OF

Mildred Tengbom

MINNEAPOLIS

MOVING INTO A NEW NOW
Faith for the Later Years

Cover photo courtesy of PhotoDisk
Cover design by Marti Naughton
Text design by MacLean & Tuminelly

Library of Congress Cataloging-in-Publication Data

Tengbom, Mildred.
Moving into a new now : faith for the later years : from the journals of Mildred Tengbom.
    p.   cm.
Includes bibliographical references.
ISBN 0-8066-3341-7 (alk. paper)
1. Tengbom, Mildred—Diaries. 2. Christian women—United States—Diaries.
3. Aged women—United States—Diaries. 4. Life change events—Religious aspects—Christianity. 5. Aged—Religious life.
I. Title.
BR1725.T36A3 1997
248.8'5—dc21
                                                                    96-52804
                                                                    CIP

The paper used in this publication meets the minimum requirements of American National Standard for Information Sciences—Permanence of Paper for Printed Library Materials, ANSI Z329.48   ∞

Manufactured in the U.S.A.   9-3341
01   00   2   3   4   5   6   7   8   9   10

*To my family
who have brought and continue to bring
so much meaning to my life,
who give me of their love generously,
and whom I love very much.*

CONTENTS

*A traveler is to be reverenced ... going from—toward;
it is the history of every one of us.*

Thoreau's Journal, *July 2, 1851*

Note to the Reader

Dear Reader:

When you glanced at the title of this book you perhaps wondered what the book was about. *Moving into a New Now* is a book about transitions: transition from a life devoted to a career to one of retirement; transition from reasonable certainty in regard to the future to one of uncertainty; transition from being in control to losing at least some of one's control; transition from effecting change to experiencing one's need of being changed.

It is a book about the changes life demands of us when we face illness, sometimes terminal; when loved ones die; when we suffer physical losses; when we give up some of our independence; when we have to make decisions about where we are going to live; and when we are faced with the ongoing responsibilities and concern for adult children and grandchildren.

It is also a book about the avenues open to us for replenishing our spiritual resources so we can meet life's sobering changes. It is a book about moving away from being obsessed about our own needs and learning to reach out in various ways and thus discovering new meaning for the latter years of our lives.

This book does strike some somber notes, but it is not gloomy. It traces the journey from passivity to response, from despair to hope, from worry to trust, from a parched spiritual life to one bursting into bloom, from wondering what meaning life now holds for us to discovering new meaning.

It guides us on the journey where reaching out, we receive; where in loving and appreciating others, we are loved the more; where in looking for and finding grace scattered throughout every day, we become grateful and contented people; where in seeking God, we find him. Finally, the book points us to a resurrected Christ who walks with us and who awaits us at the end of our journey.

Admittedly it is the story of my pilgrimage, for I lifted the entries from my journals written over six years. I realize that the pilgrimage each of us makes is unique and different, but I tried to choose and include only those situations with which I thought you, my reader, sooner or later, in greater or lesser degrees, would be able to identify.

To give you a sense of direction I added subtitles to the entries. As you journey with me during difficult days of testing you may "feel my hurt in your heart," so to provide little resting places for you, places where you can stop, reflect, and direct your eyes to God from "whence cometh our help," I have included verses from God's word or portions of hymns. Some of these were in my journals. Others I have added.

A final word. From time to time I shall refer to my family. Perhaps it would be helpful if I introduced them to you.

Luverne, my husband, can look back on a life given in service as a parish pastor, a professor of biblical studies at lay training colleges in Tanzania and the United States, and as a seminary professor in Singapore. Self-effacing, gracious, and endowed with a cheerful disposition enlivened by humor, he anchors our family to Jesus. Our oldest son, Daniel, is a missionary in East Africa. Our daughter, Judy, is a medical technologist, and her husband, Barry, is employed by the State of California in the Department of Fish and Game. They have two children, Alison and Reed, and live in northern California. Our daughter Janet, an ordained pastor, is married to Ron. At the beginning of this story they have no children and are living in St. Paul, Minnesota, where Ron is completing his seminary training. Our son David, also an ordained pastor, is married to Rebecca (Becky), and at the time my journal entries begin they have two children, Rachel and Jonathan. They live and minister in Los Angeles.

I have gathered entries from my journal to compose this book, praying that it will point you to Jesus Christ who ever lives ready to strengthen, help, and encourage us on our way.

Mildred Tengbom

Retirement and old age must, of course, be accepted.
We have to give up all sorts of things,
    and accept with serenity the prospect of death,
    while remaining as active, as sociable and friendly
      as we can,
    despite an unavoidable measure of loneliness.
We must learn
    to use leisure profitably,
    take up new interests,
    interest ourselves in young people
    and new ideas.
We must learn
    how to pray,
    how to meditate,
    how to acquire wisdom,
    how to be grateful.
For its part society must restore to the old
    their sense of their own value as human beings,
    and make them feel they are really accepted.
It must also safeguard their dignity
    by means of adequate financial resources
    and personal attention.

                  Paul Tournier, Learn to Grow Old

${\mathcal A}$CKNOWLEDGMENTS

${\mathcal T}$his book is close to my heart. It was "in" me for a long time crying out to be born long before words began to find their way onto paper. I am indebted to many that it finally is finished.

After thirty years of writing, I well know that producing a book that finds its way to bookstores is a team effort. I am deeply grateful to all who have worked with me, many whom I do not know by name. I also want to express my thanks to Ron Klug for invaluable editorial suggestions, to Alice Peppler for polishing and refining my finished manuscript, and to all the others: production editor James Satter, cover designer Marti Naughton, the design team at MacLean & Tuminelly, the marketing department at Augsburg Fortress, and the employees in stores all over the country.

My special thanks to Mary, Maxine, Karen, and other friends who encouraged me to say what I had to say directly and straightforwardly and above all write as honestly as I could. I owe my deepest gratitude to my husband for his patience and encouragement during the seemingly endless months I worked on this book.

I want to add a word of deep gratitude to the many people who may never know that I am grateful, that is, those who have written the books that I study and ponder and from which I gain insight and understanding. To them I am indebted.

With prayer I send the book on its way.

Year One

Confronting
Our Mortality

The big "C" bomb dropped.

December 3, daybreak

𝓛AST NIGHT WE LAID IN BED, my loved one's arms around me and my arms encircling him. The night was dark, and I knew darkness too.

Yesterday after Luverne and I walked out of our doctor's office, neither of us repeated the word the urologist/surgeon had uttered.

"Cancer," he had said. "Cancer in the prostate."

The word hit me with such force that feeling myself reeling, I grabbed the arms of my chair.

"We hope with surgery we can get it all," the doctor said.

I wanted him to say, "With surgery we *know* we can get it all." In fact, I didn't want to hear the word cancer at all!

At home Luverne paced like a caged lion in the zoo.

"I don't believe it!" he stormed.

"Doctors make mistakes," I said.

Luverne, distraught, had said, "I'm going to book a flight! Fly away. To Minneapolis. Anywhere."

But I knew we could not escape. In my heart I knew our doctor had told us the truth, and that made me afraid, more afraid than I ever have been.

When we went to bed, I found the hollow in my loved one's neck and burrowed my face there. I felt his tears wetting my hair, and then I cried.

In my darkness I searched for peace but found it not. Only at length did I fall asleep and then only to dream, strange dreams that have left me more frightened than ever; and so I've come here to my study to write and pray and try to find a sense of calmness for my soul while, in bed, Luverne continues to sleep.

One dream haunts me. I was trying to pick my way through a maze of bushes taller than I was, bushes with prickly branches that caught in my clothes and held me. I was bent over, struggling to carry a man who hung limply in my arms. The man was far too heavy for me to carry, but somehow I was managing, falling down, picking up my burden and myself, and struggling on.

In my dream I realized the man in my arms was my own son, but he was no longer a baby as he was when he died, but a grown man. I pushed on, headed downhill. Then through the bushes I caught a glimpse of what looked like a graveyard and began to sob: desolate, convulsive sobs that shook my being.

Crying, struggling, slipping, falling, and picking up myself again and again, I fought my way through the thorny bushes, and then in the midst of all this confusion, the dream vanished as dreams sometimes do.

When I awakened, I shook my head, trying to rid myself of the memory of the dream, but it still is with me.

Dawn is slowly parting the lids of night now. The birds outside are striking up their morning concerts. I wonder how they can sing. Don't they know?

I can't help it. Our doctor's words yesterday continue to echo back. I wonder what the days ahead will hold for us. For our family. For me.

Light is filtering into our home now, this home I love, this home which has sheltered and nurtured our four children and us.

I think I hear Luverne stirring. I must hurry in, bend, and kiss him. Tell him how much I love him. We'll hold each other again, and then it will be time for both of us to begin living another day.

Bombs explode our worlds.
December 3

$\mathcal{M}$Y SHOWER, usually so cheering, offered me no refreshment this morning. In the kitchen, making breakfast, I moved with difficulty, my legs so heavy I could scarcely put one in front of the other.

It still seems unbelievable that life could change for us so suddenly. The week had been very happy up until yesterday afternoon. Judy (special to us, firstborn daughter that she is), Barry, little Alison, and Reed arrived from Stockton Monday night. Tuesday, Luverne's day off from teaching, we picnicked at Laguna's beach, hunted for shells, soaked up the sun. In the evening our David, Becky, Rachel and little Jonathan came, and our home hummed with happiness. We adults chatted in the living room while the four little ones tumbled all over each other in our big family room, shrieking with joy. How good it had been to gather half of our brood home again!

We waved good-bye to Judy and her family Wednesday, reluctant as always to see them go. When Luverne left for school, he said, "Before I come home I have to stop at the urologist's. He wants a biopsy done on the prostate. Why, I don't know. Did the ultrasound show something they didn't tell me about?"

"Precautionary," I said. "You know how your primary doctor takes no chances. He's concerned because the score of your PSA was elevated. That's why he sent you to the urologist and had an ultrasound taken. But I don't think you've anything to worry about." I really hadn't been concerned.

When Luverne came home from the urologist's, he said, "Results on Friday."

I'd been surprised yesterday when Luverne asked me to go with him to the urologist's office.

"What we hear from the doctor could have quite an impact on our lives," he said. His anxious remarks surprised me. We didn't have anything to worry about, did we?

At the doctor's office we didn't have to wait long before the nurse ushered us into his private office. My eyes took in the room. Leather chair by the desk. High-backed, swivel leather chair behind the well-polished desk. Mahogany paneling. Oil paintings of Western scenes. Old cowboy boots frozen in metal on the floor. A sculptor of a cowboy on a horse on a stand. Live plants: tall, spike-leafed, a cactus bristling thorns.

Luverne sat down on the chair facing the desk. I settled myself on the firm, almost hard davenport.

The doctor strode in briskly, shook hands with Luverne, nodded to me. Then sitting down in his high-backed leather chair, he leafed through a sheaf of papers on his desk. Putting them down, he tipped back his chair, looked squarely at Luverne and said, "Now listen carefully to what I am going to say to you." And then he let us have it. "The tests have shown cancer."

I heard the "C" word as though from far away.

The doctor continued talking; and as he did, his voice slowly floated back into the room for me, but I found myself listening in a strangely detached, unfeeling sort of way.

"On both sides," the doctor was saying. I heard his sentences tumbling out in disjointed words. "Not large . . . not yet . . . active . . . cancer's unpredictable . . . never know, changes its activity . . . two more tests . . . CAT scan . . . entire abdomen . . . cancer metastasized . . . lymph glands . . ."

Luverne had moved to the edge of his chair, his face was flushed.

"Then bone scan . . . radical prostatectomy, of course."

"Doctor!" Luverne almost yelled, leaning forward and grabbing the arms of his chair until his knuckles went white.

The doctor continued unperturbed. "Entire prostate . . . incision navel down . . . very major surgery . . . seven, eight days hospital . . . seven days no stair-climbing . . . six, eight weeks . . . full recovery."

"I'm not going to the hospital!" Luverne exploded. "I'm teaching! I can't go!"

The doctor leaned forward in his chair, his eyes narrowing. Placing his elbows on his desk, he made a tepee with his fingers. "I've heard it all before," he said. I was hearing better now. "Over and over. A job to do. A project to complete. A trip to take. Some have done it. Then they come back to me, and I have to tell them it's too late."

"I told you, Doctor, I'm not going to have surgery."

"Listen," the doctor said, "if the cancer is contained in the prostate, the chances for cure are very good. Let it go into the lymph system and chances drop to as much as 60 percent sometimes. Once it gets into the bone," he waited a second, then said deliberately, shrugging his shoulders, "you can call your travel agent. Decide what trips you want to take. You'll have about a year to take them if you are lucky."

Luverne was gripping both arms of the chair. His chin jutted out. I looked at the doctor. His chin was jutting out too. Like a couple of roosters, I thought, cocks poised for a feather-flying fight. I still was feeling like a detached onlooker watching a drama being spun out before my eyes.

The doctor's manner relaxed. His voice softened. "You're an intelligent man."

Luverne only squirmed. "You don't understand! I can't walk out on my teaching."

"Your doctor sent you to me to keep you alive." The surgeon reached for his phone. "I think I'll have to call him to come and talk with you."

More shifting on Luverne's part. More protesting.

Then finally, to my own surprise, I found myself standing up and saying, "We have a stubborn Swede here, Doctor."

"I've gathered that."

"For once I'm making the decision." I said. "When can we set up the appointments for the tests?"

A huge smile spread over the doctor's face. Jumping up, he came across to us from behind his desk.

"I've found a partner," he exulted. "We, you and I, will work together to see this thing through," smiling at me; and as Luverne stood up unsteadily, he placed a hand on Luverne's shoulder and said, "and I will work on you."

A shiver ran through Luverne's body. Dumbly he followed us to the receptionist's counter.

"Which hospital? St. Joseph's, Western Medical? Tustin Community?"

"St. Joseph's."

"If we can. If not, can we make it Western Med? If radiation (I caught my breath and heard my ears begin to ring) will be needed, they have the best facilities for that."

Tests—Wednesday. Results—Friday. Surgery—Wednesday the 13th. We walked out.

"I'll drive," I said.

"I'm going to drive!"

I prayed our way home.

To be brought face-to-face with our own mortality so abruptly! And this is the year Luverne will celebrate his seventieth birthday. He's too young to have this happen to him.

We called the children yesterday: Judy and Barry in Stockton, Becky and David in Hawthorne, Janet and Ron in St. Paul. Dan, in Kenya, will get the news via a letter.

And so we come, O God, today,
And all our woes before you lay;
For sorely tried, cast down, we stand,
Perplexed by fears on ev'ry hand.
—Paul Eber, 1511, 1569, tr.
Catherine Winkwoth, 1829-1878, alt.

A chance find?

10:10 P.M., December 3

YESTERDAY WAS HARD. Today's been hard too. We've struggled through the day, both of us so exhausted every movement, every thought has been an effort. Waves of nausea and acute weariness have swept over me from time to time, threatening to overpower me. Then they pass only to return later. Strange.

When I walked past my wall calendar in the kitchen this morning, I sighed as I noted all the commitments I had made months earlier, some to be met either before Luverne's scheduled surgery in six days' time and others shortly afterwards. I wondered how I ever would be able to fulfill them.

After breakfast, while the clothes were tumbling in the dryer and the water was swishing the dishes clean in the dishwasher, I assembled all the boxes of Christmas decorations. Opening the first one labeled "candles," spying a strip of parchment lying on the bottom, and being curious, I lifted it out. On it Janet, during her high school years when she was designing wall plaques, had inscribed in calligraphy, "So give me the strength I need."

I stared at the words. I had found a prayer I could pray. Taking the paper, I taped it to the refrigerator door. And praying that prayer as I worked, I did manage to get most of the Christmas decorations in place for all our various scheduled festivities.

And now, dear God, I need to sleep. Please help us this night to get the rest we so desperately need.

Why are you downcast, O my soul,
Why so disturbed within me,
Put your hope in God,
for I will yet praise him,
my Savior and my God.
  (Psalm 42:11)

Routine to the rescue.
December 4

ONLY MY EARLY YEARS OF TRAINING under Mother are keeping me going.

Mother. I've thought of her so often today. As a child and a teenager I had known Mother as a woman with a carefully thought-out plan for each month of the year, each week of the month, and each day of the week, and an equally astute planned routine for the work of each day, right down to how I should move around the room while dusting so as to conserve body movements!

Furthermore, Mother not only had thought through her plan and routine, she worked them, ticking along steadily, in rhythm, like a clock that never wound down. And she saw to it that I, too, worked her plan. How I had resented what I considered regimentation!

"It's like growing up in the army," I used to fume to myself.

Years later—and aging does help one's perspective—I came to understand that Mother's organizational skills and her disciplined living enabled her to carry on when she was left a widow with dependent children.

Still later, when as a married woman myself I found babies arriving in our home every year or second year until we had four, the habits ingrained deeply in me by Mother's training stood me in good stead. And now once again they are helping me. Distracted, distraught, and confused though I am, I still can function. Habit takes over. Following a routine steadies me when all else is heaving and shaking.

The unexpected disrupts.

December 4

Aᴼᴛᴇʀ ᴛʀᴀɢᴇᴅʏ ꜱᴛʀɪᴋᴇꜱ, we try to continue with life as usual, although nothing is as usual anymore. We go to Christmas smorgasbords, visit with the people, smile, wish them a happy holiday. We attend church, greet old friends and meet a new one, sit in the service, sing, recite the creed. We come home, eat lunch, and lie down for a nap.

The usual. But nothing is as usual. The festivities tire us immeasurably. At church the word we hear preached doesn't speak to our need. We pray, but our prayers don't seem to "get through." We nap, but do so holding hands; and even after Luverne falls asleep, his hand in mine keeps twitching.

No, nothing is as usual. Luverne is on the phone, calling relatives and friends who live afar, asking for prayer.

Nothing is as usual. To a major degree I am no longer in control of my life; ordinarily I like to think I am. As Luverne's body has relayed messages, sounded warning, and urged action, it has assumed control. I resent this intrusion; it upsets my plans, introduces uncertainty into our lives, frightens me.

Nothing is as usual. Now fear is the predominant emotion within me, a shivering fear that I am unable to control. A fear I can't escape from because I feel death breathing on my neck.

"We are all fighting it—fighting the transitory, the evanescence of life, against death and the shortness of life," Anne Morrow Lindbergh wrote. "I don't think anything conquers that feeling and that fear."

No, it doesn't, Anne, at least not for me—yet.

And because of that fear nothing is as usual. As Dag Hammarskjöld wrote, "In the old days, Death was always one of the party. Now he sits next to me at the dinner table: I have to make friends with him." But I don't want to make friends with him! Thinking about it makes me angry. And then what happens? Luverne and I explode at each other for no acceptable reason. I know that when we get frightened, we can flare out in anger, but I still feel guilty that I can't handle the situation better.

Nothing is as usual. I find myself working feverishly: tackling cleaning jobs I've long neglected, and attacking them with a vengeance; but working that way, I soon exhaust my energy.

Nothing is as usual, and the saddest part is some aspects of our life might never be as usual again.

We are lamenting; both of us are lamenting; and when people lament they don't behave as usual. But lamenting itself is a natural part of being human. Can I accept this? Can I believe that although I am a broken human being, God loves me and will continue to love me? Can I believe that one day he finally will make me completely whole? Ironically, when that happens it will be through the very thing I fear now: death.

Tomorrow we'll face another occasion to live and act as usual as we host the noon meeting of retired pastors, spouses, and widows of Swedish descent. May my trembling hands and my forgetfulness not convey to them, O God, that life is not as usual anymore. We want them to enjoy the day; they have heavy enough burdens of their own to carry.

Friends to the rescue.

December 5

LUVERNE HAS GONE TO BED. I'm tired too, but grateful that the luncheon went well. How could I have handled it without friends? Ginger, pushing her walker in front of her, worked hard in the kitchen. Chris, still in shock after the death of her husband, had come to help. Seger and Ruth arrived early, and Ruth helped set up tables. How old is Ruth? Pushing 80 or close to it?

Charles Dickens, in one of his writings, quoted an old proverb: "May we never lack a friend when we need one," and then added, "and when found, make a note of it."

Tomorrow we go to the hospital to get the CAT scan of Luverne's lymph system and also a bone scan. Then we'll wait for the results.

One of God's provisions for healing.
December 6

*Is any one of you sick? He should call
the elders of the church to pray over him and
anoint him with oil in the name of the Lord. And the
prayer offered in faith will make the sick person well;
the Lord will raise him up . . . The prayer of a
righteous man is powerful and effective.*

The ancient words recorded in the fifth chapter of the book of James echoed off the cathedral ceiling of our living room as the first rays of dawn, streaming through the big window facing east, lit up the faces of those who stood in a circle around Luverne who was seated on a chair in the middle of the room.

Charles and John, our pastors, had come, along with David, Becky and little Rachel, and Becky's parents, whom Rachel always refers to as "Big Grandma and Grandpa" (we're the "Little Grandparents").

Little Rachel, standing holding her mother's hand, watched with questioning eyes as one by one those present laid hands on her Little Grandpa's head. I saw her edge closer so she could peer and see her Big Grandpa slowly pouring something from a little dish onto the head of her Little Grandpa; and then all the people closed their eyes and began to pray.

I was crying, not noisily, just tears running down my cheeks; but seeing my tears, Rachel edged closer to her mommy. I could see she wasn't sure what all this was about.

Now her Big Grandpa was speaking again:

*May the Lord bless you and keep you;
May the Lord make his face shine on you
and be gracious to you,
The Lord look upon you with favor
and give you peace.*

Little Grandpa was standing up now and the people were hugging him and Little Grandma and saying good-bye.

"Why do we have to go?" she asked her mommy.

"Little Grandpa has to go to the doctor," Becky said.

"Why?" Rachel asked. "He doesn't look sick."

Taking control.

December 6

$\mathcal{H}$OW DOES ONE—how shall I—get through the onerous task of waiting? Waiting to get tests done, waiting for the results of the tests, waiting to have the surgery over. The questions buzz around my head like bees. I try to back away, but they persist in circling round and round my mind as we sit in this dismal, dimly lighted waiting room, waiting for Luverne's name to be called for a bone scan and a CAT scan of his lymph system.

We arrived here early as requested, and we have been sitting here for over an hour. Chairs line the room and another two rows fill the center section, all those chairs positioned to face a wall-hung TV which first flashed us a depressing newscast and now blares into our ears one of those endless, banal talk shows.

People have come, checked at the reception window, sagged into chairs, heard their names called, disappeared through the one door to reemerge later and leave. Why haven't we been called?

How I hate waiting! I've never been good at it, and sitting here with nothing to do, the worrisome questions nettle me. What if the cancer already has metastasized? What if it already is in the bones? What if the doctor can't get it all?

Memories of friends who died because cancer invaded their prostate glands surge back. I try to pull the shade down over those memories, but the cord for the shade keeps slipping out of my hand, and the shade slides up.

In the case of one friend, that sneaky, traitorous cancer found a cranny in the brain, nestled there, and began to grow. The last weeks —or was it months?—of his life he lay blind. I've never had the courage to ask his wife the extent of his suffering during those final weeks—I've protected myself. Perhaps one day I shall ask and weep. Good heavens! Here come the tears again! But he meant so much to me; he was both friend and mentor.

Our other respected friend, during his last year, spoke of pain, white-hot pain and red-hot pain. In some divine way he was able to embrace his pain and suffering; and in doing so rejuvenating and reproductive life flowed through him to others.

As a snowbird he flew to winter in the Southland. We had visited him in his mobile home. Residents in the mobile court told us about the Bible class he taught.

"To begin with just a few came," they said, "but soon the numbers who attended grew and grew. They grew and grew. Conduct a Sunday morning worship service for us, we begged. So many people came to that service that soon two hundred people filled the hall. We set up chairs outside, and people came and filled them. New hope was born in our hearts as we listened to him. And some of us found our way back to the God we had known in our earlier years."

Ah yes, my mind knows that many have found grace to climb out of despair and rise above pain and suffering, but my whole being rebels against the thought of my—of our—having to do it. I'm a coward in dealing with pain. So when I think of our two loved friends and Luverne and ask, "What if . . . ?" I find myself clenching my fists and yelling, "NO! NO! NO!"

I must stop this nonsense right now! I have no business projecting myself into a situation that might not develop. I must not imagine what might not happen. Instead, I must take each day, each hour, each fraction of each hour as it comes, and in quiet waiting before God I must seek to be at peace with God "and in the noisy confusion of life keep peace with my soul."

Help me, O my God! My faith is in doubt!

After Luverne's tests

We WAITED THREE HOURS just to begin Luverne's tests. Finally, after numerous trips to the receptionist's window to make inquiry, someone came out and called for "Dr. Teng."

"Tengbom?" Luverne asked.

She looked at the clipboard. "Oh, sorry, Dr. Bom," she said.

"Tengbom," Luverne repeated patiently.

"Oh," she said. Then, "We have some emergency cases so we will take care of your bone scan first. Follow me."

A nurse injected something, then addressing Luverne said, "Now you must drink lots of water."

"But I was told not to drink before my CAT scan."

"You are going to have a CAT scan?" Off she went to check. Back she came. "We will work it out somehow. Drink some but not too much."

More waiting. More glasses of goop to drink. More waiting.

Morning faded into afternoon and afternoon was headed for evening when finally at four o'clock an aide told us we were free to go home. A whole day spent in the hospital waiting room and most of that time merely waiting! And now we have to wait to learn the results.

The day the doctor told us he had discovered cancer was an evil day. Today was another evil day. Nothing to distract us; too much to frustrate us, and too much vacant time to worry—even as I write these words I scold myself, asking how I can so quickly forget the sacred time at our healing service this morning. O foolish, foolish Millie, to call this an evil day! Forgive me, O my Savior!

A final word from the devotional reading, a word from Howard Thurman, a pillow on which I can rest my head: "To walk in the light while darkness invades, envelopes, and surrounds is to wait on the Lord. This is to know the renewal of strength. This is to walk and faint not."

Thanks you for those words, dear Jesus. Continue to give us the strength, faith, and, patience we need.

Who gets our ear?

𝓐LONE IN MY STUDY AGAIN. How thankful I am Luverne has no trouble sleeping even these days.

My *Guide to Prayer* has designated Psalm 205 as one of the readings for this evening. The question asked is: what discipline is God urging me to practice if I would be at peace? This is what I glean from the psalm.

- Every morning and every evening I do wisely to give thanks to God for specific blessings.
- I am to remember the wonders God has done in the past.
- I am encouraged to tell others how God has helped me.
- I am to look to *God* for strength.
- I am counseled to look for God in all that is happening to us.

In C. S. Lewis's *Screwtape Letters* the senior devil said to the junior devil something about how few things surpass anxiety in its power to block God. And as I remember it, the Devil told the junior devil to be on the watch because God wants people to be concerned with what they do but the devil's business is to keep people worrying about what might happen to them!

But if I am to concentrate on *doing* something, if I am to walk away from worry, anxiety, and fear and instead work toward you, dear Lord, and faith and trust in you, I need your help, day by day, hour by hour.

Adequate rest is important.
10:05 P.M., December 9

𝓑USY, BUSY DAYS. Friday David came and helped Luverne put up the Christmas lights outside. Little Rachel had come with her daddy, and she had a wonderful time opening all the boxes that contained the lights. She can be quite a little actress too and beams with pleasure when we burst out laughing. As David said, "Little kids offer us the best therapy we ever could hope to find anyplace."

But even with Rachel's helping us get through the morning I've never seen Luverne as tired as he was by noon. David said the same. I was glad I had prepared a hearty lunch; and after eating it, Luverne laid down and rested and said he felt better.

In the evening about thirty adults from our church came for hors d'oeuvres, first stop for them as part of our annual adult Christmas progressive party. Afterwards Luverne and I drove to church where all the groups had gathered for the main course, but we excused ourselves from the dessert and coffee which was being served in other homes. Too tired.

The teeter-totter tilts up.
December 11

LUVERNE'S PRIMARY DOCTOR PHONED this afternoon that he had received the reports of Luverne's tests. Wonderful news! No malignancy any other place than in the prostate! We quickly phoned Judy, Janet, David, and our friends who had gathered for the healing service.

Teetering.
8:30 P.M., December 12, home alone

TODAY HAS BEEN SUPER STRESSFUL. Luverne has been running around, trying to take care of everything he thinks needs care: watering the lawn and garden, softening the water for the house, sending off insurance claims, getting money out of the bank, vacuuming the whole house. I could feel myself catching his nervousness. We've lived together so long that I can't divorce myself from his feelings.

We were to report to the doctor early this afternoon and then be prepared for Luverne to be admitted to the hospital. The doctor saw us only briefly. It still being early in the afternoon, we decided to go to the cafeteria for tea. Tried to browse through the newspaper. Difficult to do. Both of us strung too tight. Decided finally to go to admitting and get the process over with. That was the beginning of the most frustrating part of the whole day.

First we were told Luverne was not to be admitted until the next morning, then told to wait while they checked with our doctor, then told to wait until they cleaned a room. As we were getting settled in the room, a nurse bustled in.

"You might as well understand right away that times have changed," she said. "We're understaffed with nurses. We can give most attention only to the dying and care for your most pressing needs. We work twelve-hour days. Everybody's short-tempered," and then she disappeared. She needn't have added her last remark.

Not even a pitcher of water appeared until six o'clock and Luverne's evening dinner didn't come until eight. The young attendant who brought it saw Luverne sitting dressed in pajamas and lounging robe and said, "Wow! Look at those sexy legs!" Really!

I left the hospital after Luverne had finished picking away at his dinner and came home. A few minutes ago I took Daniel Simundson's book, *Faith under Fire*, off the shelf, and these words spoke to me: "It is easy to believe in God when things are going well. It is another thing to continue coming to him when the going gets rough . . . this is the point when [some] give up their dialogue, or they are so frightened of God's reaction that they never tell him what they really want to say."

And then Simundson goes on to say that "even words of doubt expressed to God become statements of faith, because they are addressed to the right person." Do I dare believe this?

I'm afraid, Lord. I need you.

9:30 P.M.

*D*AVID JUST CALLED. He's coming from Los Angeles to spend the night here and go with me to the hospital tomorrow. Thank you, Lord. Be with Luverne in the hospital tonight. Be with David and me and all our family. Help us to trust you.

Reliving the day.

December 14
The day after Luverne's surgery

$\mathcal{D}$AVID AND I ARRIVED EARLY at the hospital yesterday. As I walked down the hall I wondered how we would find Luverne. Worried? Anxious? Fearful? Instead, as we stepped into his room he surprised us by greeting us with his big, broad smile.

"The most wonderful thing happened," he said in a rush. "Around 5 A.M. I was awake and suddenly felt a warmth sweep through my whole body, draining away all my worry and anxiety. I could actually feel it leaving me. And then the most incredible peace filled my whole being. I can't explain it. Nothing like this has ever happened to me before. It was wonderful. Still is."

I stared at his face. Positively radiant, I thought. Aglow, almost translucent, as though a light within is shining through.

A sob behind me caused me to turn around. David was crying. And then I saw him swallowing, and the muscles around his mouth constricting as he struggled to compose himself.

"I was awake, Dad. Felt you had been plunged into a well of fear. I started to pray God would set you free from your fear, raise you up. Prayed about fifteen minutes, and then felt released, as though I didn't need to pray anymore."

The aides had been standing quietly, respectfully in the hallway. Seeing me look their direction, one of them questioned me with raised eyebrows. I nodded, and they came in.

We followed as they rolled Luverne on the gurney to the holding space outside the operating theater. It was the first time I had seen it from an upright position. Two other gurneys, positioned parallel to the wall, bore white-sheeted occupants who appeared to be already unconscious. Eerie, I thought, almost morgue-like, hoping Luverne couldn't read my thought. A state of un-being was the way I always had thought about being anaethesized; I never had been able to submit to it without trepidation; I always had hoped and prayed I would wake up again.

Luverne's doctor stepped up to the gurney.

"Take me away, Doctor," Luverne said. "I commit myself into your hands and the hands of God. I have absolutely no fear."

The doctor looked momentarily startled at this changed man, then smiled. He glanced at David.

"Our son David," Luverne introduced.

The doctor extended his hand, shook it heartily, then placing an arm around David's shoulder he said, "You take care of your mother; I'll take care of your dad."

The aides pushed open the doors to the surgery, wheeled Luverne inside, and the doors swung shut.

"Why don't we go and get you some coffee, Mom?" David said.

"I'm glad you're with me, Dave."

"Don't worry, Mom. Dad'll be all right."

I hope so, I thought. *I wish I had some of that wonderful peace Luverne talked about.*

When we returned from the cafeteria, we found Rhoda, Elder, Helen, Charles, Woody, Gerry, and John gathered in the waiting room. We sat silent, I gathering strength from their presence.

Midway through the surgery a green-gowned, green-slippered, green-capped surgeon padded up to us.

"We've removed the prostate," he said. "Good news. It appears the cancer was contained in the organ."

"Did the surgeon have to cut the nerve?" I asked.

His voice softened. "I'm afraid so. We couldn't risk anything else." He paused. "I'm sorry . . . but all is going well. He'll be all right."

The surgeon disappeared and I headed for the chapel. After a while the door opened softly, and one of our friends came in and sat down beside me. I put my head on his shoulder and cried.

Cried because of relief. Cried because of loss. Cried because our lives together would never be the same again. Oh, the loss—the irreplaceable loss! Never again to experience the most intimate way a man and a woman express their love for each other! Inconsolably I sobbed.

I'm not sure my friend knew why I was crying. I only know his arm around me was as welcome, soothing and comforting as warmed pajamas on a cold winter night.

My friend did not probe. I did not confide. With some, one enjoys a friendship of intimacy, sharing, and confidentiality. With others, one appreciates a friendship of restraint, reserve, and respect. God, in his dealings with me, has taught me I need both—with and from him and others.

I groped in my bag for more tissues. My friend, gently releasing his arm around me and leaning over, handed me a box from the table.

"Come back to us when you're ready. We'll be waiting for you," he said. "And, Millie, remember. Often the future looks bleaker than it really turns out to be."

And he left me alone to pray.

Prayer time two evenings after Luverne's surgery . . .

Endings Come Hard

O God of Eden and God of Cana's marriage feast,
 in the beginning you created us male and female.
You gave to each a body,
 a gift to be accepted,
 a presence to be welcomed by the other
 so love could be celebrated.
But now, O God, in my woundedness I cry out,
 for our turn has come
 to be stripped of this power.
The life we knew before which so fully satisfied
 is no more.
Touch our wounds gently with a healing hand, O God.
Gift us with graces of acquiescence, resignation,
 acceptance.
Enable us to come to terms with the toll of aging.
Aging is simply part of our living.
Slowly I am coming, not only to accept this as normal,
 but to receive it into my heart.
Help us then as we lose the bits and pieces of life,
 to focus

not on what we have lost,
but on what still remains.
Bless, O God, this one I love so much.
Bless the thinning hair,
the walk still so quick,
the memory sharp, unfailing,
the humor ever present.
Bless him in his kindly spirit,
his unselfish eagerness to help others,
his firm convictions.
Bless my loved one, O Lord,
and bless us in our touching and caressing,
in our whispered words of love,
and in our long-stretched-out hugs and thirsty kisses.
Bless us in our conversation,
in our eating and in our drinking,
in our sleeping and in our dreaming,
in our laughing and in our crying.
Bless us in our playing,
in our traveling,
and in our dozing in our chairs,
for the inevitable, the unavoidable has now visited us,
and through your grace, O God, and with your help,
we shall seek to accept and tacitly embrace it.

Made to measure.

December 16

MY DEVOTIONAL READING for this morning contained this quote from Helmut Thielicke:

What we meet with in our life is not so terribly important; the only important thing is whether we accept it as coming from God's hand and whether we dare to trust that it was made to measure—your measure and mine—and therefore is exactly right.

Encouragement has a role to play.
December 19

A WOMAN AT CHURCH YESTERDAY said she felt my book *Grief for a Season* had been written for her. Words like this keep me writing, difficult though circumstances to do so may be—impossible now, in fact.

It troubles me a little, however, because I always feel rewarded when others tell me something I've written, said or done has helped them. C. S. Lewis wrote in *Mere Christianity* that we must get over wanting to be needed and that some "goodish people" find this the hardest temptation of all to resist.

And if it is God who blesses and helps others, then why do I feel "up" if I hear someone has been helped, and "down" if I hear nothing?

And yet . . . and yet, I know myself well enough to know I *do* need affirmation and encouragement.

Coming home for Christmas.
December 21

*T*ODAY WHEN LUVERNE CAME HOME I was grateful for the large patio doors on ground level leading into our family room which will be Luverne's abode for the next several days. The doctor has ordered no stair-climbing. I am thankful also for the bathroom on ground level.

During Luverne's recuperative time downstairs the wide patio doors will usher in sunshine and a view of our orange and lemon trees, boughs bending with heavily laden fruit, and our pepper trees whose trunks wind around each other as though in embrace.

Closer in are the heavenly bamboo, the ficus and the miniature palm trees, the bushes and roses that will burst into bloom later, as well as the bedding plants I'll tuck into the earth when spring has warmed the soil and rain will fall.

In a few days, after Luverne has gained some strength, the fireplace nook will offer a cozy space where friends can put their feet under our table and together we will enjoy a simple but hearty soup, salad, and homemade bread supper, and later in the family room we'll continue our conversation as we enjoy dessert, coffee, and tea. I look forward to all this speeding up Luverne's return to health. I am more than ready to leave behind our strenuous days of living with a life-threatening illness, absorbing anxiety, and patience-taxing waiting. I want to hasten toward living a life less stressful.

It is evening now. Luverne is asleep downstairs, and I am in my study upstairs again, feeling grateful for so many things. I find my heart lifting up in worship of my God, and the words of a hymn written in the 1800s by Adelaide Anne Procter begin to spill out. During my late teens and early twenties I sang the hymn often, and now in my elder years I find myself returning to it.

> *My God, I thank Thee who has made*
>   *The earth so bright,*
> *So full of splendour and of joy,*
>   *Beauty and light!*
> *So many glorious things are here,*
>   *Noble and right.*
> *I thank Thee, too,*
>   *that Thou hast made joy to abound;*
> *So many gentle thoughts and deeds*
>   *circling us round;*
> *That in the darkest spot of earth*
>   *some love is found.*
> *I thank Thee more that all my joy*
>   *is touched with pain,*
> *That shadows fall on brightest hours,*
>   *that thorns remain;*
> *So that earth's bliss may be my guide,*
>   *and not my chain.*
> *For Thou who knowest, Lord, how soon*
>   *our weak heart clings,*
> *Hast given us joys, tender and true,*
>   *yet all with wings,*

So that we see gleaming on high
Diviner things.
I thank Thee, Lord, that Thou hast kept
    the best in store;
I have enough, yet not too much
    to long for more.
A yearning for a deeper peace
    not known before.

The space beside me in bed will be empty tonight also but no matter. The house no longer is empty. My beloved has come home for Christmas.

Christmas: dependency, gifts, and joys.

10:00 P.M., December 25
I am alone in my study.

SOME MAY SAIL UNEVENTFULLY through recovery from prostate surgery; Luverne hasn't. His incision opened this morning, and so this day, Christmas, found us back in the emergency room getting it stitched together. After I had tucked him in bed at home once again, I set out to find a pharmacy open. Finally I found one, and then wandered up and down an unfamiliar aisle trying to inform myself about each of the various kinds of sanitary pants offered.

It was Christmas Day. I felt resentful that we had not been told we might need these so I could have been prepared and wouldn't have to spend Christmas Day in this way.

I'd never paid any attention before to this aisle in a pharmacy. *Depend.* I stared at the printing on one of the boxes. That's what illness does to us, I thought. Makes us dependent. And to lose control of one's bodily functions—even if only temporarily—and be forced to wear diapers—who wants that?

Well, I finally bought something and went home.

Then this evening, trying to make the best of a not-so-good day, I built a fire in the fireplace. Plugging in the lights on the Christmas tree, lighting the other candles scattered throughout the room, I slid in our CD a disk of carols. Turning the volume low, I went over and sat down on the edge of the bed beside Luverne. It was, after all, the evening of Christmas Day.

The sweet, smoky smell of logs burning began to seep into the room. The candles flickering shed a soft glow.

We sat silent, holding hands, listening to the fire crackle and the choir singing.

"Joy to the world! The Lord has come!" the singers burst out.

Ah, yes, centuries earlier God had come to us in a way that would change all life for us. A helpless, dependent baby had been born to give us hope for life after death. Through prayer, skilled surgeons, and surgery, God had come again to give us hope for extended life for Luverne on earth. And sitting there I could feel Luverne's love traveling across to me. My heart overflowed with gratitude.

Luverne broke the spell by asking me to go up to his room and get a package out of his socks drawer. I brought down a small box wrapped in gold paper.

"Open it," he said.

Inside the black velvet box lay a gold band and set in it seven diamonds that sparkled in the firelight. Reaching in and lifting it out, he slipped it on my finger. My tears wet his hand. What a checkered, but in the end, happy Christmas Day it has been.

Half an hour later prayer time brought these words from Malcolm Muggeridge which fell on me like a gentle benediction:

> *In the stress of life, it is always open to us to wait on God. All we have to do is, as it were, make a little clearing in the wild jungle of human will, and then keep our rendezvous with our Creator. He is sure to come; His presence falls like a comforting shadow, and then we are at peace.*

Great is God's faithfulness.
December 31

$\mathcal{J}$ANET AND RON HAVE BEEN HOME and returned to St. Paul. They had been married in Minneapolis in August, and long before we had any inkling that Luverne would undergo surgery, we had laid plans to fly them here after Christmas for a reception so their friends could greet them. We had sent out invitations, received replies. That reception, to be held in our home, was one of the social events that had loomed formidably before me after we learned of Luverne's cancer.

But once again friends came to our rescue. Ron and David carried Luverne upstairs to our bedroom to clear space in the family room. Luella did the catering, and her creations were far more eye-appealing than any I could have prepared. Dee baked a second wedding cake. Joyce, Karyn and Helen set up tables and "skirted" the serving tables, then went home and, exquisitely dressed, reappeared to serve as hostesses, tending so graciously and attentively to everyone's needs I was free to visit with the guests.

Janet brought home and wore her wedding gown. Off and on during the afternoon some of the men slipped upstairs to visit with Luverne. And so quietly did my friends work that when the last guest left, the kitchen was completely in order, the leftover food put away, and I wasn't even tired.

This morning I stood in front of our fridge and looked at the two slips of paper taped on it. One had the list of all the planned social events of Christmas, and every one had a line running through it, signifying completion. The other slip was the parchment with the words, "So give me the strength I need."

Once again I had tasted the faithfulness of God. Strength had come through God's word, through prayers, through letters, cards, phone calls, and the presence of friends and family and also through the practical help they gave.

Breathing a prayer of thanksgiving, I ripped off the door the paper with the crossed-out items. The prayer I left on the door. Who knows? I just might need it for the year ahead.

Sometimes we are catapulted
into disaster with a suddenness that paralyzes
the mind and leaves the exposure to fear unshielded by
courage or by strength. . . .

The issue of our spirit and the thing that
confronts us is joined—we are engulfed in the
great silence of fateful struggle. It seems that nowhere,
in no place, can an answer be found. In vain we seek
a clue, a key, even a little thing to give a fleeting respite,
a second wind. Again and again it is apt to happen: the
miracle of relief; a chance word from a casual conver-
sation; a sentiment or a line in a letter; the refrain of
an old song; an image from the past; a paragraph
from a printed page; a stirring prayer in the heart—
the miracle of relief and we are released. . . .

It is good, so very good, to experience the
quiet ministry of the living spirit of the living God.

—*Howard Thurman,* The Inward Journey

The steadfast love of the Lord, never ceases,
his mercies never come to an end;
They are new every morning;
great is your faithfulness.
(Lamentations 3:22,23)

Year Two

Searching for and Gathering in Grace, Trust, and Courage

Newly found joys.

January 10

I ASKED A FRIEND how they spent Christmas this year.

"Life's changed for us," she said. "Our children are scattered. Their work schedules are tight. Plane fares are high. We're alone now. Two years ago we began volunteering to cook and serve Christmas dinner for the homeless." Her face broke out in happy smiles. "We've never enjoyed Christmas more."

Faithless fears.

January 12

*T*HE AGING BODY'S ABILITY TO HEAL and renew itself cheers me, but for Luverne little nuisance complications have slowed down the process. I brought him to the hospital yesterday for surgery to correct bladder problems. Minor surgery, the doctor said. Is any surgery minor for the patient?

I'll bring Luverne home tomorrow, but tonight the house echoes with emptiness. Outside the wind, whipping up a storm, intensifies my feeling of desolation. If Luverne were to die first, how would I be able to continue to live? I ask myself. I know I shall, but still I tremble when I think about it. It never has been easy for me to give thanks to my God when his demands become austere, I, who love the easy route, to live with darkness, I, who love the light. To steady myself I turn again to the passage for this evening, trying to let it speak to me.

> *Strengthen all weary hands,*
> *steady all trembling knees,*
> *and say to all faint hearts,*
> *Courage! Do not be afraid.*
> *Your God is here.*
> (Isaiah 35:3-4)

I flip ahead the pages and note these verses underlined during another time of testing:

Long before you call,
I shall answer; before you
stop speaking I have already
heard you. Rejoice and be glad!
(Isaiah 65:24,18)

No ear has heard, no eye has seen,
what God will do for those
who trust in God's love.
(Isaiah 64:3)

I shut my Bible. Do not distress yourself with imaginings, Millie. You're tired and feeling lonely. Put all in God's hands and then sleep and rest. And with that I shall crawl into bed, comforted but still feeling lonely.

Transcending one's own concerns.
January 15

1 WOKE UP THIS MORNING feeling as though I hadn't slept even though I knew I had. Later, as I was writing a letter, a phone call interrupted me, the disturbance making me feel really crabby.

But surprise! The chaplain at one of our hospitals was calling to tell about a program he is introducing to train fifteen chaplain associates who will offer hospitality and respond to the spiritual needs of patients and, as appropriate, refer patients to him or other clergy. He will provide intensive, thorough training for a three-month period, then assign the volunteers to specific floors for visitation and continue to offer ongoing monthly training. He wondered if I would be interested in becoming a volunteer.

I was so surprised all I could say was, "Well . . ." and then I asked if I could call back in three, four days. He agreed.

Sitting alone here in my study in the quiet of the evening, I've been thinking and praying. From other times of personal testing I've learned the importance of moving beyond oneself and one's own concern. I thought I recalled something Viktor Frankl wrote about reaching out. Scanning my bookshelves, spotting the book, taking down *The Unheard Cry for Meaning*, and paging through the book, I located the statement:

> *. . . being human is always directed and pointed to something or someone other than oneself; to a meaning to fulfill or another human being to encounter, a cause to serve or a person to love. Only to the extent that someone is living out this self-transcendence of human existence, is he truly human or does he become his true self. He becomes so, not by concerning himself with his self-actualization, but by forgetting himself, giving himself, overlooking and focusing outward.*

What, O God, are you saying to me?

Seizing the courage to venture out.
January 18

THE CHAPLAIN CALLED THIS MORNING, and I accepted his invitation.

Learning something new stimulates one.
January 19

WE MET WITH THE CHAPLAIN this evening for our introductory session. We're a mixed group from many churches. Next week a doctor will speak to us about the disease process.

Dying by inches.
January 22

M ARGY IS SLOWLY DYING, Margy, my cherished friend, my confidante, and not only my friend and my confidante but friend and confidante of many others, a "mother-in-Israel," in the spiritual sense.

I hate the cancer that relentlessly is destroying her piece by piece. The night fourteen months ago when we kept vigil with her husband while the surgeons performed brain surgery to relieve the pressure that would have killed her otherwise remains grooved in my memory. We had waited outside the surgical theater from four in the afternoon until two in the morning when a surgeon, still clad in his greens, walking wearily in, told us the surgery was palliative, not curative.

Surgery extended Margy's life, and in doing so, I suppose, for the immediate time it was palliative, for my dictionary defines palliative as meaning "to reduce the violence of." The cancer did not kill her then. But the surgery didn't end her suffering. How greatly she has suffered! Suffering has wearied her; even eating requires immense effort. Pain twists her body and pounds in her head so brutally that without the strongest medication the doctors can prescribe I think it would drive her insane. Often even the medication cannot mask the pain, and then she can only lie and moan.

"I wish I could die," she has said to me again and again.

When she's been bed-bound I've sat beside her often, once in a while reading to her, but more often I've just sat there, holding her hand, wordless, wishing I could relieve her pain and suffering but helpless to do so.

The last months, however, I've found myself visiting her less often and staying only for a few minutes; not because I have felt pressed for time, but because I have felt so compressed with anxiety I have nothing to give her. I have protected myself also—selfishly—because I already am hurting so much I don't want to hurt anymore. I feel terrible about this. Of course, I know many others are ministering to her, but this doesn't absolve me of guilt. I wonder how much longer Margy will have to wait to be relieved of her suffering.

Half an hour later

DURING MY QUIET TIME I read from John Baillie's *A Diary of Readings* a sentence by Richard Rothe that eased my feelings of guilt: "God does not require that each individual shall have capacity for everything." Thank you, God.

Stress intensifies aches and pains; water therapy comforts.
January 23

LUVERNE IS GAINING STRENGTH but still experiences some discomfort. Errand running eats up much of my time. My knees and back are hurting, my body telling me to slow down. Exercising in the pool would help, but I can't find time to go to the pool.

Everyday tasks are sacred.
January 24

THIS MORNING WHILE IT WAS STILL DARK I drove to the hospital to sit with the family of a friend undergoing surgery. I stayed until nine, did marketing, and at eleven friends surprised us by dropping in. I invited them to stay for lunch. Luverne had a doctor's appointment this afternoon. As we were walking into the doctor's office, we met a friend walking out. The doctor had not given her an encouraging report; I listened and hugged her.

Later this afternoon the phone rang. The ambulance had taken the wife of a friend to the hospital. We called our friend at the hospital. It sure would be nice to have you here, our friend said. We left immediately.

My article for *Guideposts* lies on my desk half-finished. It's impossible to find islands of uninterrupted time when my own inner spirit quietens enough so I can work reasonably well.

"The will of God is also manifest to us in the duties and responsibilities of our common everyday life," my devotional reading this morning reminded me, but I confess I sometimes allow the will of God to become burdensome and irritating. I've done so little writing since we went to Singapore and returned that I feel like a moulting hen, not laying any eggs, a bit testy in temperament and needing new feathers.

"The great thing, if one can," C. S. Lewis wrote in one of his letters to his friend Arthur Greeves, "is to stop regarding all the unpleasant things [and, I would like to add, all the tedious chores—Lewis had a housekeeper!—and all the intrusions] as interruptions of one's 'own' or real life. The truth is, of course, that what one calls the interruptions are precisely one's real life—the life God is sending us day by day." I agree, but I'm a slow learner.

Telling it as it is can lead to peace.
January 26

$\mathcal{W}$E PRACTICED LISTENING SKILLS at our chaplaincy session last evening, using questions given to us. As I listened to different ones role-playing the patient, I thought back to my experience following the death of our second baby, the answers I gave and the answers I would have given if I had dared to answer honestly.

Had I been asked how God was working in my life right then my response probably would have been silence.

My honest answer would have been: "He is making life utterly miserable! Unbearable! For the second time I've lived through over seven months of feeling sick, nauseous, worried, being confined to bed for days at a time, terrified by false alarms, shakily hopeful when things quietened down, and now at the end, what do I have to show for it? Another small grave, that's all!"

Had a chaplain asked me if being sick had made any difference in my feelings about God, I would have evaded an answer and replied I hoped in two, three days to be feeling fine. My honest answer would have been: "I'm mad, downright mad! I had prayed and prayed and believed as hard as I could and look what happened! God invited me to pray. Promised he would hear. What a cheat he's turned out to be! Says one thing and does another. Do you think I'm going to risk trusting him again?"

At the same time I would have lain trembling, wondering what God would do to me having made such blasphemous remarks. If the chaplain had asked to read the Bible to me, I might have answered, "Thank you, Chaplain, that is kind of you, but not today, please. I've had many visitors and am tired." My honest answer would have been, "NO!"

"Isn't prayer important to you?" the chaplain may have asked, and I would have assured him I couldn't live without it, while in my heart I would be thinking that it used to be, but I wasn't sure how much praying I'd be doing anymore.

If the chaplain wanted to know if there was anything that would make my situation easier, I would have assured him we appreciated all he had done for us. My honest answer would have been: "Yes, keep people away from me, all who want to tell me everything I did wrong, or who tell me God means this for my good, or I must have done something to displease God, or I wasn't careful enough, or God saw I wouldn't be a good parent—I don't want to hear any of that crap. Keep them away from me! That would help."

If the chaplain had concluded by wondering what about God was important to me in my present situation, I undoubtedly would have glided through that saying it was God's faithfulness. I would've told him I knew God was with me, that in the end he would make everything work for good. I was sure he would. I was trusting him. He always had been so good to me. He never had let me down.

My honest reply, accompanied by tears, would have been: "Yes, yes. I can't give up on God. I can't live without him. That's the distressing thing. I can't live with him, and I can't live without him. But I hope he won't leave me. Please pray he won't abandon me. He must be around someplace, don't you think, though I can't see him just now? He's never treated me this badly before. O God, why did you do it? I can't understand; I just can't understand!"

I hadn't answered the questions honestly then, and I had hated myself for my double-talk, my lack of honesty. If I had responded honestly, I undoubtedly could have been helped. Instead it had taken years to break free, to dare put into words how I actually had felt, to experience again God's presence, to be able to offer petitions, to trust him. What a long, long journey it had been! I wonder if the patients I visit will dare to be honest with me?

Stunned into silence by death.

January 29

*I*N THE DARK I GROPED FOR THE PHONE that kept ringing and ringing. It was Chin Young, our Korean friend. Edwin, Chin Young's husband, Luverne's colleague and friend and David's golf companion, had died during the night. Only three days ago Chin Young and I had chatted over lunch, untroubled by any premonition as to what was about to happen, and now Edwin was dead!

Hurriedly we pulled on clothes. I drove, Luverne eating the bowl of cereal he had grabbed on the way out.

Chin Young was standing in the open doorway, watching, waiting for us. I opened my arms; she walked in. We stood silently hugging each other and crying.

Chin Young's younger brother, having dismantled and folded back the hide-a-bed where Edwin had been sleeping since climbing the stairs had become difficult for him, was vacuuming the carpet.

We did what we could, dialing the numbers of Ed's family, contacting their pastor, driving Chin Young to the mortuary, doing all those things that need to be done at a time like this and which can be difficult for the shocked and grieving ones who move as though in a world other than the world of reality. At 3:15 P.M. we drove home to do some more phoning for Chin Young, ate a sandwich, drank some milk, and then drove to the mortuary to be with her until nine.

Whenever I stand in the presence of death and look at the now lifeless body of one whom I have loved, I know, in a strange way, that what I am seeing is not the one I loved. The loved one truly has "departed," as we say. Death faces us with a solemnity, a mysteriousness, a profundity we experience no other time. Death always leaves me wordless.

The stabilizing effect of rituals.

February 1

THIS EVENING LUVERNE WASN'T FEELING WELL, so I went to Edwin's funeral service alone. Walking up to the front, I sat down.

A fresh bereavement often threads me to the many times in the past when one of my loved ones has died, and so at funerals I often find myself grieving again their deaths. But my grief now is tempered; it is not as sharp or charged with questions as before, and it also is softened by gratitude.

Sitting there waiting for the service to begin, I thought how just a year ago to the day I had been called upon to both grieve and rejoice on the same day, because that was the day my sister had died—how I miss her!—and also the day our little granddaughter Alison blew out her first birthday candle. Death and birth had been set together in close proximity for me as I witnessed the closure of one life and celebrated a year of new beginnings for the other. The day had asked me to perform some emotional gymnastics on the uneven parallel bars.

I heard soft rustling behind me now as people moved into the sanctuary and took their places. Edwin had outlived many of his friends. Could it be also that after Edwin married Chin Young some friends perhaps felt awkward and uncertain in how to cross cultures? Sad, I think. We miss so much if we don't try.

The strains of the organ broke out solemnly into the processional hymn. I watched as our David, one of six ushers, escorted the coffin followed by Edwin's son and daughter and their families, Chin Young, and a nephew of Chin Young's who is living with Chin Young while he attends school here.

Processions, I thought, provide a symbolic activity for the bereaved as they accompany the body of their deceased loved one into and out from the sanctuary for the last time and then to the cemetery where the bereaved, in walking away from the burial site, mark the separation taking place. The refreshments or common meal after the service also provide symbolic activity for the grieving family as they enter the social hall—but this time without the one who used to enter with them—to be received into the circle of the living.

At that point in my thinking the pastor interrupted me as he invited us to move into the service by joining in a liturgy of responses. As I followed it, I discovered once again that the liturgy was providing me with a sense of order and structure I need in this world often appearing to be confusing and chaotic.

After the liturgical responses we sang, hymns of faith and hope we sang, and listened to the comforting, reassuring words of God as scripture was read. I soaked it all in.

The eulogy traced the faith journey of one who had sought to follow Christ and in doing so the value and worth of Edwin's life was underscored. Pastor Egge, an old-time friend, recalled how many years ago Edwin had asked him to conduct the services for Edwin's twin sons who had drowned.

"What shall I say?" Pastor Egge had asked Edwin, knowing three, four hundred young people would be sitting in the congregation, observing, questioning, listening.

"Edwin thought for a few minutes," Pastor Egge remembered, "and then said, 'Tell them God does all things well.'"

As the service continued with the pastor directing our attention to God who would continue to be faithful in supporting the bereaved, I experienced peace wrapping itself around my heart; and I hoped Edwin's family was experiencing this too.

Because the cemetery lies many miles away from the church, we'll lay Edwin's body to rest tomorrow. Then Chin Young has invited the family and a few close friends to gather for lunch with her in a private room in a restaurant. Chin Young understands the value of ritual and symbolic activity.

Mosquitoes that buzz and annoy.
February 4

LUVERNE IS BACK IN THE CLASSROOM teaching part-time, attending meetings, filling up his appointment book. Life as usual for him, I think, but not for me. After one—or one's loved one—has had an encounter with a life-threatening disease, accident, or illness, some things change. For me, life has assumed a tentativeness it did not have before. I am restless. Decisions I have resisted making in the past now command attention from me; questions that formerly I had pushed to the back of my mind now insist on claiming my attention.

Luverne soon will be 70. When will he retire from his teaching position at the Institute? We both have been blessed in being able to work at vocations we love; and retiring from a job one has loved can be difficult, I know. The temptation may come to wonder what meaning life can hold afterwards, but doesn't the time come when we need to walk away from the podium, the computer, the desk, the farm, the office, the pulpit—wherever we've pursued our career—and instead discover new interests?

We need to decide where we want to spend our later years. How long do we want to continue living in this 3,000-square-foot house? Clean it? Repair it? Live in this neighborhood? Do we want to wait and move until our physical strength will be diminished, until we will find it difficult to make friends in a new setting? All these questions nag at me daily while Luverne, thankful that his surgery was successful, continues working as usual.

I wouldn't want to voice it to anyone, but some retirement communities I've seen have made me shrink back, because I've feared—rightly or wrongly—that I would stagnate in them. Maybe that's because I'm too young for them. But I would like to get settled somewhere so I wouldn't have to move again; after living in twenty-one different places for shorter or longer periods during my life, I don't want to move again EVER!

These last days I've thought of one place that would interest me: Pilgrim Place in Claremont, only thirty-five or forty miles from here, founded especially for missionaries, although other Christian workers live there now also. I've thought of Dr. Mildred Winston, who had walked us around the campus pointing out all the attractive features. Last night I sat down and tried to recall them.

- Attractive campus. Roads wind around, most homes refreshingly different in architectural style, yards well-groomed.

- Homes varying in size from tiny one-bedroom ones to a few four-bedroom homes.
- Independent living in a rented house as long as one is able to care for oneself.
- After that, move into an apartment unit, play lazy, get your meals cooked, room(s) cleaned, and laundry done.
- When and if needed, a full-care unit on the campus.
- Entrance fee a percentage of one's assets.
- Noon meal in common to provide for sociability and at least one well-balanced, nutritious meal daily. (I could enjoy not cooking; Luverne prefers to eat at home—conflict on this point.)
- Book clubs, support and special interest groups. Lectures and seminars on social action and justice, health and welfare, women's special concerns, international relations—can't remember them all now, but more than enough to keep one mentally alive.
- Music to enjoy. Chorale, recorder, and chamber music groups perform. Play-readers too.
- A "young" community. People are encouraged to enter at age 65 or earlier and cannot enter after 75.
- Sense of community develops as everybody works in one way or another for the huge Pilgrim Festival in November when people come to purchase paintings, woven goods, lapidary, wooden objects, ceramics, vintage clothing, stamps, coins, used books, sweets, bakes, candy, old silver and china, linens artifacts, and more, all produced, fashioned, or gathered by Pilgrims. Proceeds?—can't remember how much, about $120,000, I think, or was it more—provide subsidies for those whose financial resources have shrunk, thus granting a measure of financial security to needy residents.

Well, that day way back those many years ago, we'd been so impressed that we had taken Mildred's advice and had filled out application blanks. I guess the year Luverne would turn 65 had seemed eons away.

However, 65 did come but with it a short-term call to Singapore which we accepted with alacrity, and we had moved ahead our requested date of entrance. And after returning from Singapore, it's been so easy to settle into life as usual again that we almost have dismissed the thought of moving.

But isn't it time now, I reason with myself tonight, to be talking seriously about the future and be prepared to move if a house becomes available? Actually, we'd be lucky to get in; we've been told the waiting list is unbelievably long and only a small number gain entrance every year.

The trouble is Luverne doesn't want to discuss it. Whenever I bring up the subject, he swats it away as though it's an annoying mosquito. How can we reach a decision that will please or at least be acceptable to both of us?

Troubled, I turn to a prayer in our *Book of Worship*:

> *O most loving Father and God,*
> *you want me to give thanks for all things,*
> *to fear nothing except losing you,*
> *and to lay all my cares on you,*
> *knowing you care for me.*
> *Help me to do just that, O my God.*

The mosquito punctures.

February 11

MARGY DIED TODAY.

The mosquito punctures again.

February 15

AS SOON AS I HEARD the garage door open, I hurried out.

"Honey," I said, not trying to conceal the excitement in my voice, "the associate director of Pilgrim Place called this morning saying they might have a house with two bedrooms and a study available for us the first part of May."

Luverne had reached in the back seat to get his briefcase and was taking longer than usual getting it out.

"Didn't you hear me, Honey?" I asked. "A house, a house big enough so we each can have a study, might be available soon."

Still no answer.

His head finally emerged from the back seat; his face, when I could see it, looked as stricken as it had when the doctor had told him his prostate had a malignant growth in it.

I felt my mouth drop open. I said no more. He strode into the kitchen. I followed him. He headed into the dining room, then the hallway, and I heard him climbing the stairs.

What am I to make of this? Didn't we agree long ago that eventually we would retire at Pilgrim Place? Or did he agree thinking the time would never come? Or is it that he isn't ready yet? And if not now, when?

Misdirecting our anger as we grieve.
February 19

LAST NIGHT AT MARGY'S MEMORIAL SERVICE I was so miserable. With Margy's dying I have lost an irreplaceable friend, the one to whom I could go when I have been confused, troubled, or concerned, the one who has said little, but listened well, the one who has touched or, when I have needed it, held me, the one who at the end has said, "Shall we pray?" The dictionary defines comfort as giving strength to, to afford a sense of security to, to ease grief or trouble, to offer hope. Margy did all this for me, because praying with Margy drew me into Christ's presence; I then could draw strength from him or feel his strength being released in me. No one will ever be able to replace Margy for me.

I feel guilty also because lately, visiting her, I have breezed in and out. Ever since I learned she died with only an employed caregiver by her side, my guilt has deepened. "How could you do this?" a little voice accuses me. You, who with your training know how much it means to dying people to have loved ones by their side. Where were you when she needed you?

I did share my anguish over this with a friend; and she said, "But, Millie, no one of us could know exactly when Margy would die. If we had known, all of us would have been there." But that hasn't eased my guilty feelings.

I also have felt cheated because I had no opportunity to say good-bye to her. As soon as I heard about her death, I went to her home only to learn that her body already had been taken away for cremation. I was angry. If only I could have seen her one last time! Stood beside her, wept over her, thanked her, asked her to forgive me, wouldn't it have helped? Of course, I know Margy wouldn't have been there, but in her dead body at least I could have gotten as close to her as I could. I know many people don't feel a need to say good-bye in this way, but I do.

I wonder, did this contribute to what happened next, because just before we left for the Memorial service Luverne and I had a blowup. The memory of it is still painful for me.

I was at fault. I introduced the subject of moving, because days before I had overheard a phone conversation in which Luverne promised to continue teaching part-time until the end of the school year. Are we going to be wedded to the college for life? I had fumed. I was still simmering on Saturday, and so just before leaving for church, I exploded.

"I want to move," I said. "I want a smaller home on one level in a community where all levels of care will be available if we need them."

Luverne said nothing. I continued. "I don't want our kids to worry about us if we get sick or disabled and wonder where we can be cared for. And I want to move NOW while we're still fit and young enough to cultivate new friendships."

Luverne said we still had plenty of time.

And then I said I thought it was time I be given the opportunity to make the choice. All our married life I gladly had gone along with him wherever he wanted to go, which was only partly true, because we've made all our decisions together.

Luverne's face flushed. He looked as though I had slapped him, and it was my turn to feel stricken. I collapsed on a chair, withdrew into myself, feeling isolated from him, incredibly lonely, and sad, sad, sad.

At this point our grandfather clock had struck the half hour, alerting us it was time to leave for the Memorial Service. We rode in silence to the church, I sitting in the front seat but as far to the right as I could.

In church I sank dismally into a back pew; and when Dave, Becky, and Rachel came, I moved over so they could sit between us. I glanced at my watch. The service wouldn't begin for another quarter of an hour.

I was so, so miserable. I knew I didn't want to make a decision to move based solely on what I wanted. But with mind upon mind and will upon will clashing, how could we come to unity? And isn't unity what we women want—even on a global scale? But how does one attain unity when people cling to differing opinions and convictions?

And wasn't my reasoning, my judgment worthy of Luverne's thoughtful, unbiased consideration? I asked, feeling angry again. I sighed. Being a woman is hard work, I thought. Since childhood, growing up as the peer sister to three brothers, I struggled to consider myself as having equally as great value as they. I have continued to tussle with this in my adult life and especially whenever I have erred by comparing myself to others. And now I found myself struggling with it again.

Why was Luverne so hesitant to move? Was he afraid if he did, he wouldn't be happy? He would be as happy as he chose to be, I thought stubbornly. I sighed again. I believed Pilgrim Place would help provide an environment that could enrich both our lives, but I also did not want to achieve my desires by fighting. Then I was losing my distinctiveness as a woman, wasn't I? I was assuming the aggressiveness of many men; and don't I, as a woman shrink back from aggressiveness that leads to strife, estrangement, and violence of any kind?

A women's trio singing "Come to the Water, Stand by My Side" brought me back sharply to the occasion for which we had come to church. Margy had died! Now I couldn't even talk over these things with her! My loneliness increased, so when I heard the words, "I know you are thirsty, you won't be denied," I broke down and began to sob.

"I saw every teardrop and for those tears I died," the trio sang on, and my tears fell faster and wetter.

Little Rachel, peering at me and unable to understand why Grandma was crying, crawled into Becky's lap, hung on tightly to her, and continued staring at me. I wanted to stop crying for her sake but couldn't.

Becky slipped an arm around me; then Luverne, stepping across the others, sitting down beside me, put his arm around me, but I could derive little consolation from his offer of tender comfort. All that I could do was cry and cry, relieved I was in the back pew. Oh, if I only could find a woman to talk to who would understand me!

Asking for help.
February 24

1 PHONED MY FRIEND KAREN TODAY. Karen is twenty-five years younger than I, but the first day we met at a writer's conference about twenty years ago we both knew we were meant to be friends.

"Karen," I said, "I need to find someone to give me a sense of spiritual direction. I'm so mixed up about a number of things that I feel like a puzzle put together by a child."

We talked for several minutes and then Karen said, "I know just the right person. Sister Viktor at the Center for Spiritual Development in Orange. Phone for an appointment."

Phone a stranger? Do I dare?

The listener.
February 26

1 DROVE TODAY to the Center for Spiritual Development to meet with Sister Wiktor, whom Karen has recommended. After we were seated in an uncluttered, peaceful, private room, she asked me why I had come. This Sister has the bluest eyes I've ever seen, and she looks directly at a person when she speaks.

I hesitated momentarily and then told her I'm hungry, thirsty, weary. I said I had been reading Henri J. M. Nouwen's book, *Reaching Out*, in which he wrote about a period of dryness he had experienced; and how he had understood once again the importance during such times of learning to become quiet so when we read the Word of God, we can hear God speak. But he believed it could be helpful also to find someone who could give direction to our journey, a spiritual director, a mentor. I told her that thought was new to me.

Sister Vicki waited.

I said Nouwen noted that when all kinds of confusing voices speak to us both from outside and within, we easily are tempted to make our desires, God's desires, our will, God's will; and so we need someone to encourage us, to guide us, perhaps even to caution us as we seek to find our way.

Then she wanted to know why I had come to her.

I told her one of my friends, attending one of her seminars had received help, and so I phoned for an appointment with her. The blue eyes, still looking directly at me, were so friendly, so hospitable, so kindly I felt no urge to avert my eyes when I spoke to her.

Then she asked me to tell her what was going on in my life that was troubling me, and I told her Luverne and I couldn't agree about where or how to spend our later years. I told her about my sister dying and Edwin and Margy, and how guilty I felt that during Margy's last weeks I hadn't spent more time with her.

Sister Vicki is such an attentive, caring listener I kept on talking and told her how Luverne has begun to lose his hearing, and then I told about his cancer surgery, and then—I hadn't expected to say anything about this—but I began to blurt out that sometimes I felt so frustrated because I had hoped our retirement years would bring peace and quiet of mind and heart, lessened responsibilities, and with those the energy and enthusiasm necessary to give myself seriously to writing, and instead all this other has happened, and I can't write at all!

I heard myself saying I've felt as though I'm running a race with the laces of both my shoes tied together, as though I'm running a race looking at the backs of all the other writers, and I'm afraid I'll never be able to realize some of my dreams.

After getting all that out, I stopped, stared at the wall, bit hard on my teeth, blinked fast, and struggled for composure.

Leaning over, touching my knee gently, Sister Vicki said, "If the tears want to come, let them come."

After a few minutes I told her when I had to face the possibility that Luverne's life might come to a quick end, I had faltered, staggered, reeled, and my faith had grown shaky; but when I had tried to share this with a close friend, she only said, "I'm surprised at you, Millie," and that hurt.

Well, I kept on until finally I felt emptied out. Then my new friend spoke, and she said my losses have been many, cumulative, and varied, which frequently happens during our later years. They have called for different responses, but she suspected their very frequency probably has not allowed me time to absorb and process them.

Loss always depletes and wearies us, she said; and when we have to store our losses up inside, we feel the weariness even more. She thinks it's time for me to take time for Millie, and she said she was giving me permission for that. And finally she asked if I would like it, she could offer some directives for guided reading. I told her I thought that would be great. And then we prayed. As we parted, agreeing to meet again the following week, she enfolded me in her arms.

I walked out feeling lighter than I have for months; and as I drove home, I reflected on what Sister Vicki had offered me: a caring presence, an assurance of acceptance, and with it a felt reminder of the presence of the suffering Savior, of the Father of all comfort, and of the life-giving power of the Holy Spirit.

Do prayers of confession fall too glibly from our lips?
8 P.M., February 28

1 AM BACK HOME from the all-day Ash Wednesday retreat Sister Vicki suggested I attend. I found the retreat center, although in the heart of the city, set far enough back from the streets and surrounded by enough trees so traffic noise doesn't disturb.

Our director proved to be a woman about fifty, I guessed. She gave her name and spoke briefly about her background. Then she asked us to go around the circle, giving our first names and sharing something that has been meaningful to us in our walk with God or tell what expectations we had brought with us to the retreat. When we concluded, she asked us to spend time in silence, each one giving thanks for specific gifts of grace we have received the past week, month, or year.

Closing my eyes to shut out the unfamiliar room and those around me, I waited. Sitting in the silence, an amazing variety of "graces"—many I would not have thought of mentioning ordinarily—streamed into my consciousness and flowed out of my heart, surprising me, delighting me and leaving me feeling deeply loved by God and others. I couldn't believe it when our leader announced our half hour of silence had passed.

She then went on to introduce the second section; and as she spoke, phrases I had heard as a child during worship services, floated back, reminding me that "because I was a poor sinner, by nature sinful and unclean, and guilty of having sinned against God in thought, word, and deed," I needed to "draw near with a true heart and confess my sins."

In introducing the next part, our director asked us to search our hearts deeply, asking for light and allowing the Holy Spirit to probe. Then we were to write ten times we have despised our soul.

At her words I found myself stiffening. Could not introspection and self-examination become morbid?

I glanced around our circle, then finally, reluctantly picking up my pen, I wrote slowly, feeling as though I was stripping myself naked as I wrote.

Ten Times Have I Despised My Soul

The first time was when I spoke critically of another and did not nail it down as jealousy or bias; when I criticized instead of finding something in the other to affirm or praise.

The second time was when I, in my heart, arrogantly considered myself superior to another.

The third time was when I was part of a group discussing a certain issue, and I did not voice my convictions; not only because I dislike and shrink from confrontation, but also because I was afraid I would be ridiculed, if not at that time, later as little clusters discussed our conversation.

The fourth time was when I excused my lack of discipline in my own prayer life.

The fifth time was when I verbalized words of forgiveness but left crannies in my heart for birds of resentment, ill feeling, and an unforgiving spirit to build a nest.

The sixth time was when I became angry when someone criticized me and could not be humble enough to ask if the criticism was justified.

The seventh time was when I was dishonest and assuaged and smothered the guilt I felt by telling myself that everyone in a lesser or greater degree is dishonest.

The eighth time—and all the other countless times— was when I have not trusted God, have not believed he is in control of my life and will make everything work for good in the end, but instead I have allowed doubts to overwhelm me.

The ninth time was when I spoke hastily in judgment before I had learned all the facts.

The tenth time was when I evaded hearing the stories
of those whose lifestyle differs from mine both because
I am capable of being opinionated, and also because
I do not want to reexamine my views and beliefs.

I looked at my list and thought sadly of all the other things that I could add.

We took time out for lunch and relaxation. A bell summoned us back. We spent the afternoon in guided meditation, silence, and praying, each of us on our own responding, thanking God first for forgiveness, then trying to listen to what God might be wanting to say to us in our present circumstances. Almost an hour must have passed before the director announced a short break. When we reassembled, our director told us to choose from the table in front a piece of cloth, a chopstick, and a plastic twister and fashion a small knapsack. Then passing around slips of paper she asked us to write those qualities of character or those sins we don't want to carry in our knapsacks.

After all the reflection and praying I had been doing, I found it easy to write several things:

- my impatience with Luverne when I thought he was slow in making a decision
- the times I had spoken unkindly to him
- my trying to minimize the pain he was feeling as he considered quitting teaching
- my preoccupation with myself and my work that sometimes prevents me from not being more genuinely, fully, and sympathetically interested in the cares, concerns, and joys of our children
- my self-centeredness that has ways of popping up
- the anger and bitterness I had felt when Margy died

On and on I wrote until my little plaid knapsack bulged. While we had been writing, the director had been lighting a fire in the fireplace.

"Bring your knapsacks here, empty them of your papers, and burn the papers," she said.

One by one we found our way to the fireplace and stood watching our papers curling up and crumbling into gray ashes.

"Now I would like you to fill your knapsacks with the character and personality qualities that you want to become part of you this Lenten season."

Once again we wrote. When our pens were stilled, our director led us in closing prayer, together we prayed our Lord's Prayer, then bidding each other good-bye, we parted.

Minutes later I swung our car onto the main street, then a few blocks down the road, accelerating, I pulled onto the freeway, the cars whizzing by me, the steady din of traffic drumming in my ears, and ahead of me, brake lights occasionally flashing red, alerting me.

As I pulled into our driveway, I heard the grandfather clock inside our house striking the hour, reminding me it was time to prepare the evening meal. My day at the retreat had been blissful. Now it was time to take up again the duties and responsibilities life asks of me.

The bell tolls again.
Ash Wednesday, late evening

*J*ANET HAS JUST PHONED from St. Paul.

"Mother, have you heard? Evey died today."

Evey, my friend of over forty years, my friend with whom I had shared my first years on the Nepal border. Though miles have separated us most of our lives, whenever we have met, we always have been able to pick up and go on from where we left off.

First it had been Paul, Evey's husband's brother; then Jonathan, Evey's husband; and now Evey—three of my most cherished friends. Together, years ago, we heard Christ's call to discipleship, together we made our commitments. The memory of Jonathan and Evey's wedding in the foothills of the Himalayas when I was Evey's bridesmaid sweeps back over me. I remember when their first daughter was born.

When Paul died, he left a huge gaping hole in my life that has never been filled. When Jonathan died, I felt part of my connection with my earliest years in the Himalayas severed. Now with Evey's death that connection, in some respects, has been severed completely. I had some memories in common with those three I have with no one else: trips we took together, picnics, treks in the Himalayas, singing, reading and discussing books together, even arguing with each other. Jonathan often seemed to delight in teasing me by playing the devil's advocate whenever I stated an opinion. Sometimes I felt like taking him by his shoulders and shaking him; but since he died, even that quality has become endearing to me. But now Evey's death has severed my connection with this period. I have no one left with whom to share memories.

When I sensed God beckoning me away from my original call to Nepal and instead respond to Luverne's love and marry him and then later go, not to Nepal, but to East Africa, Paul, Jonathan, and Evey, ever flexible and open to the Spirit's leading, supported me in my decisions. Evey even had given up attending the ceremony when Jonathan received his hard-earned master's degree in education in Colorado to come to Minneapolis to attend our wedding. That meant so much to me.

And then I've been thinking of the special gift of grace all three gave me which I have cherished most of all, which has met one of my deepest needs; staunch, sturdy belief that with God's help I would be able to do anything to which I felt him calling me. And now all of them are dead! Will any other friends prove as faithful as they were in all these respects?

Why did this news have to come after the wonderful day I spent at the retreat center? What are you saying to me, O God? Are you wanting slowly to wean me away from many of my closest friends? Is it because you want to draw me closer to you?

I'm shivering and need to crawl into bed. I hope Luverne will stir when I do and awaken. I need him: his shoulder, his arms around me to ease the sense of losing. I need to cry. If I'm going to get any sleep at all tonight, I need to cry first.

Whispering in the dark.

March 1

1 WOKE UP THIS MORNING CRYING as I thought of Evey. This afternoon when I met with Sister Vicki I told her about Evey.

"So many of my friends have died within such a short time span," I exclaimed. "It's as though they had been lined up in a row like dominoes and someone pressed the first one, and now the rest are tumbling, one by one. I walk around asking why I am left. I find it so difficult to get quiet when I sit to pray."

"I can understand," Sister Vicki said. "You are going through a very stormy time."

She didn't say, "Try this," or "Do this," or "You should be able to get quiet if you really tried." Instead she said simply, "I can understand," and she allowed me to find it difficult. I wanted to hug her.

But again tonight I'm struggling. O God, I whisper, it's too much! Too many have died in too short a space of time! I can bear no more.

> *If you but trust in God to guide you*
> *And place your confidence in him,*
> *You'll find him always there beside you,*
> *To give you hope and strength within.*
> *For those who trust God's changeless love*
> *Build on the rock that will not move.*
>
> *What gain is there in futile weeping,*
> *In helpless anger and distress?*
> *If you are in his care and keeping,*
> *In sorrow will he love you less?*
> *For he who took for you a cross*
> *Will bring you safe through ev'ry loss.*
> —*George Neumark, 1621-1681*

The inaudible voice veiled in silence.
March 3

LAST NIGHT AT OUR CHAPLAINCY SESSION as we paged through sixteen pages of medical terms, nurses interpreted them for us. Without question I'm entering a bewildering new world where other caregivers speak a language I'll have to learn if I am to understand the patients' charts. How long will it take me to learn all the unfamiliar words and abbreviations?

The nurses spoke about therapy treatments offered, problems they encounter, and the pressures under which they work.

Following that a physician talked to us about the Durable Power of Attorney document, that little piece of paper which filled out and signed will give instructions to our health-care persons as to what we want in regard to resuscitation or life-support. Our chaplain urged us to fill out one and also ask our family members to do so. We left, paper in hand, a sobered group.

I drove down the hospital parking ramp and at the corner turned onto the main street now almost completely emptied of cars, past darkened buildings with only a filling station on a corner or a 7-11 store showing some signs of life. The night was incredibly quiet; the stars above shone brightly; everything was peaceful except my soul.

"Why is it so hard for me, O God, to accept the fact that one day I shall die?" I cried as I drove slowly home.

I heard no answer.

The significance of greeting cards.
March 5

I'VE SPENT THIS AFTERNOON sorting through boxes, because I know if and when we move, we'll have to de-accumulate. One of the boxes contained cards we've received. When I opened it, I thought of how Mother had said, as she was stripping down, that one thing she didn't want to part with was her cards. After tonight I think I understand why. Rereading the messages, I've felt loved, and that has brought comfort.

And then this afternoon a letter came from Karen, one of my young readers whom I've never met and most likely will never meet. She wrote that she didn't know me very well, mostly through my books, but she wanted to tell me she loved me; and then she added she hadn't told that to anyone else on earth except her parents.

Thank you, God, for your love which embraced me in a special way today through little Karen.

The need for new friends in our later years.
March 6

I'VE BEEN REREADING *Learn to Grow Old* by Paul Tournier, the Swiss psychologist. He points out that if we do not continue making friends during our later years, we may soon find ourselves without any, because former friends may move away or die.

If we moved, we would need to seek new friends. Friendships, however, are not born whole. Friendships start from a base of recognized but scattered bits of commonality and often take years to bloom and flower. Developing friendships calls for investment of time and energy. We still have both. Ten years from now it might be considerably more difficult, so wouldn't we be wise in moving now?

At the same time, one of the most wrenching aspects of moving will be living at a distance from our old friends and visiting them only occasionally. Can we hope to develop the same degree of intimacy and feel the same sense of security with new friends? Our new friends gained in our later years will be known to us only in their aging; we'll never know what kind of persons they were in their prime.

How can we know the answer? I'm beginning to sense that for many various reasons the aging person experiences loneliness. Perhaps this will motivate me all the more to concentrate on developing a deeper intimacy with Jesus.

Just allow God to love you.
March 8

"*I* STILL FIND IT DIFFICULT TO CENTER DOWN, to meditate, to get quiet," I complained to Sister Vicki when we met today.

"You've been going through a very stormy time this past year," she said. "Calmness and serenity don't come immediately and especially when a person is trying to learn it under stress. Some things that might help: designate a special chair for your prayer time, light a candle, focus your thoughts on a painting, listen to music. Later I'll introduce you to one of Ignatius's secrets, using our imagination to enter into scenes and meeting our God there. Remember also," she said, smiling, "you're just beginning. For now, quit trying so hard. Instead sit quietly and say to yourself over and over, 'God loves me, just as I am now, not because I am a good person or because I try to follow him or because I have learned to concentrate when I pray, but he loves me even as a mother loves her child. Because of this I can feel secure.' Sit. Just allow God to love you completely."

Can one such as I who sometimes try so hard to succeed in learning some things do just this? Let God do it all for a change?

Rocking on the rocking horse.
March 11

*T*HOUGH MINOR PROBLEMS CONTINUE, Luverne's cancer threat seems to have disappeared. I'm breathing easier. Strangely enough, perhaps because of this, some days I too feel reluctant to move. I say nothing about this to Luverne, of course. He doesn't need any further encouragement to continue letting life flow as usual.

Letting tears and laughter mingle.
March 12

"*I*S ANY PLEASURE ON EARTH as great as a circle of Christian friends by a fire?" C. S. Lewis wrote. (I've been dipping into his books frequently these days and making notes of statements that speak to my heart.) I thought of his remark last night after I snuggled into bed.

Longtime friends Joyce and Paul had come for a fireside supper. We reminisced about Edwin and the teaching years together Paul and Luverne had enjoyed with him.

As our conversation wandered to other subjects, we found ourselves laughing heartily. Once I wondered briefly how we could grieve during one hour and the next hour burst forth in laughter.

But if we could not both rejoice and weep, how could we survive? The complex nature of life calls on us to both weep and laugh. As C. S. Lewis noted in his *Reflection on the Psalms*, "A little comic relief in a discussion does no harm, however serious the topic may be."

Streams in the desert.
March 13

1 NEEDED TO GET AWAY from the city to open spaces where my eyes could sweep wider vistas, my mind could gain perspective, and my spirit absorb silence; and so taking a picnic lunch and a couple gallons of water, we headed for the desert. We left shortly after seven and after two and one-half hours arrived at the gated entrance to the Joshua Tree National Monument.

The desert can be forbidding and dangerous, but it also can offer comfortable silence and soothing stillness. Today only on the oases where palm trees have found sufficient water to grow did I hear soft rustling when a gentle wind blew through them.

The twisted gray rocks, the black boulders, the multi-hued exposed granite monoliths always remind me of the cataclysmic upheavals that took place in the ages past. I look at them and think of all the physical changes that have taken place on this our planet. Again and again change appears to be the thread of accent woven into the fabric of life.

In contrast to the towering rocks the fragile desert flowers bloom among the smaller rocks here and there on the desert floor, their vivid colors commanding attention, their waxy blossoms caged in and protected by prickly cacti.

There's so little movement on the desert! After the early morning hours even most birds seem to disappear; and aside from an occasional lizard noiselessly slithering by, seeking refuge in the shade of a cool rock, or a roadrunner, its towering, narrow tail held stiffly aloft, its powerful legs moving like pistons as it hurries across the road, we saw no other animals or snakes.

It's so quiet! Not even many human noises intrude, no telephone, no TV, no traffic hum. On weekdays few people prowl around the desert, and today even the few campers and rock climbers we met seemed to talk less. Luverne and I fall into silence also—just naturally. We enjoy merely being with each other, the two of us together away from everybody else.

We drove slowly until we came to one of our favorite spots. Parking the car, we took off hiking down a trail, clambering over rocks, taking time to search for, stoop, and wonder at the beauty of the fragile, transitory blooms of the desert.

At noon we found shade in the shadow of a huge rock and sat down to feast on peanut butter and banana sandwiches, milk still cold from our little ice bucket, and crunchy wine-red apples.

As the sun began to slide toward the horizon, we left the park driving slowly, took a different route home, and discovering a small family-owned restaurant in a village, stopped for a bowl of homemade soup, bread still warm from the oven, and—feeling absolutely wicked as we did it—finished off our supper with a huge piece of home-baked apple pie topped with ice cream, which, to alleviate our guilt a little, we divided.

We arrived home both tired and rested, I, quietened in spirit, and better able to see beyond what has happened these past months and believe in a future where my God eventually will work all for good. God has done so in the past. Can I not believe the same for all the tomorrows ahead?

What a gift of grace today has been! Thank you, God.

This is my Father's world; I rest me in the thought
Of rocks and trees, or skies and seas;
His hand the wonders wrought.

This is my Father's world; Why should my heart be sad?
The Lord is king, let the heavens ring;
God reigns, let the earth be glad!
—*Malibie D. Babcock, 1858-1901*

Accepting unexpected turns in the road.
March 14

THE ASSISTANT DIRECTOR of Pilgrim Place called this morning to say that a couple already resident in the community who have been living in a smaller home has stated their desire to move into the large home that she had thought she could offer to us.

They have priority, she said. We shall have to wait.

I hung up the phone and stared out the window, not seeing but thinking. What shall I make of this unexpected development? Has it happened because we need time to recover a little from all the other losses we've experienced because of the deaths of so many of our friends? Do we need time to accustom ourselves to the reality of actually moving? At any rate, I shall try to do what Henri Nouwen encourages me to do, to receive with hospitality *all* the events in my life, making space for them, not wishing they were not there or would mysteriously vanish, but rather allowing them to shape and influence me.

Does God hurt only to heal?
10 P.M., March 16

PAIN, PAIN, PAIN TONIGHT! Our chaplain had asked a doctor and a psychologist to speak to us about grief and bereavement and ways to be of assistance to the bereaved. All went well for me until the psychologist began to speak about the death of a child being one of the most intolerable bereavements, sometimes considered even more traumatic even than the death of a spouse.

"This includes the loss of a stillborn or a premature baby who lives only a short time," he said. He went on to talk about the need for parents to see and hold their babies. So articulate was he that I felt his words like a serrated knife slicing open my old wound that had been gouged out thirty-six years ago when our first little son, born prematurely, died, followed a year later by the death of our second wee son. At the time, although I had begged to see and hold my babies, doctors and nurses strongly had advised against it, saying it would be better simply for me to picture them as I had imagined them!

"Your baby is skinny and scrawny and blue," one of the nurses had said brutally. "You don't want to see him."

The little ones had been buried while I was still in the hospital. Afterwards I asked Luverne repeatedly to describe them to me, but the longing to hold them, weep over them and caress them has never ceased. I am, after all, their mother. Thus tonight, as the doctor spoke, I began to hurt so terribly I felt like crying out, "Stop! Please stop! This is hurting me!"

Finally I could bear no more. Getting up, running out, I reached the women's restroom just in time to be sick. Connie, one of our volunteers, following me, found me leaning against the wall struggling for composure.

"You all right?" she asked.

"Just memory," I gasped.

"Take your time," she said. "When you are ready, come back."

When I returned, our group was taking a break; and when we reassembled, our chaplain said, "Millie, would you like to tell us your story?"

I did, with tears. When our group disbanded for the night, one by one, coming over to me, they hugged me—all except our young friend who wrestles with the problem of suffering. I caught a glimpse of her face as she walked out the door, her jaws clenched, her eyes fixed.

Luverne was asleep when I came home. Still too disturbed to sleep,

I did this journaling, and then I took C. S. Lewis's book *A Grief Observed* from my shelf. This paragraph in particular speaks to my heart tonight.

"The terrible thing is that a perfectly good God is in this matter [i.e., suffering] hardly less formidable than a Cosmic Sadist. The more we believe that God hurts only to heal, the less we can believe that there is any use in begging for tenderness. A cruel man might be bribed—might grow tired of his vile sport—might have a temporary fit of mercy, as alcoholics have fits of sobriety. But suppose that what you are up against is a surgeon whose intentions are wholly good. The kinder and more conscientious he is, the more inexorably he will go on cutting. If he yielded to your entreaties, if he stopped before the operation was complete, all the pain up to that point would have been useless. But is it credible that such extremities of torture should be necessary for us? Well, take your choice. The tortures occur. If they are unnecessary, then there is no God or a bad one. If there is a good God, then these tortures are necessary. For no even moderately good Being could possibly inflict or permit them if they weren't."

Help me, dear Jesus, to be able to clutch this to my heart. And now for some quiet music as I crawl in bed. Thank you, Jesus, joy of our desiring, for today.

The miracle of birth.
March 23

 THE CALL CAME FROM DAVID while Luverne was teaching a class. He was taking Becky to the birthing center, he said. We left as soon as we could, arriving an hour later to find Becky's parents already there, busily amusing Rachel and Jonathan. Then, wouldn't you know it? the birthing process slowed down. Becky suggested we go and eat. We were taking the last bites of our hamburgers when Becky said quietly she thought she better get back to the center.

"Take Becky and go!" Luverne cried, looking more excited than David.

At the birthing center we could hear water running as it filled a humongous bathtub. We waited and waited. Suddenly the door at the end of the hall flew open and David called out to us. We tumbled all over each other running down the hall, but we got there the baby had slid out.

Jonathan and Rachel, squealing with delight, hopped up and perched on the far rim of the tub. Picking him up, David cuddled their little son, then held him out to me. Cradling him in my arms and stroking his hair soft as a goose feather, I crooned to him.

"Where did you come from, O Little One?" I whispered, bending my face so my cheek could touch his. I guided his tiny, perfectly formed fingers around my forefinger.

"It's like it just happened all over again for me," I said to Becky, experiencing the past merging into the present.

Reluctantly I surrendered the tiny bundle to David, then stood studying his face. What dreams was he dreaming for his new little son? Of how they would throw basketballs together? Compare the achievements and skills of baseball players? What prayers was he praying? What father-pride was stirring in his heart? What tender feelings for Becky were causing him to love her even more?

Tonight, after Luverne and I came home, we looked at each other and laughed, and then we hugged and embraced with tears.

When is it time to quit?
March 24

$\mathcal{D}$EAR GOD, source of all creative outpourings, troubled I am. Aside from my heart's outpourings in this journal, days, months, even years have passed with little else flowing from my pen.

"Are you still writing?" a young person asked yesterday.

"Not much," I said.

"I understand," he said. "When one gets old, the creative juices dry up."

I could have socked him with my fist! But I wonder. Maybe he *is* right, I think.

And then unexpected things happen, like at our conference meeting today this visiting professor, coming over to the table where I was sipping coffee as I skim-read a recent publication by an author I know, asked if he could join me.

"Of course," I said, thinking perhaps the second chair at my table was the only available one there in the Koffee Korner.

"I want to commend you on your fine writing," he began.

I almost choked on the swallow of coffee I had taken.

"I've read many of the articles you have written, and all the ones, I think, that have appeared in our church publications."

I think I stammered something; I can't remember.

"I hope you continue writing," he said.

"Thank you," I managed, and then, "Have you seen this book? Just published. I know the author. She's good."

We came home and found the usual junk mail, advertisements, and solicitations for donations stuffed in our mailbox.

"Here's a letter for you from Pennsylvania," Luverne said. He was standing by our kitchen table sorting through the pile.

"Pennsylvania? Who do I know in Pennsylvania?"

I took a paring knife and slit open the envelope.

"Honey, you're not going to believe this! This lady writes she was changing planes at LAX recently and had a few minutes to find an Orange County directory and located our names and address. She says she has been wanting to write me to thank me for my books. I can't believe this!"

So what do I make of all this, Creator God? Do I dare believe the creative juices will flow again, the muse return? But then the doubts come. What if this doesn't happen? Can I then loosen my grip, unclasp my fingers, let go of unrealized dreams? Turn to something else? O, forsake me not, O my God!

The need to stay alive as long as we live.
March 25

*W*E VISITED A FRIEND TODAY living in what I've always thought of as a retirement home. I came away with ambivalent feelings, thankful that the home provides all the excellent, skilled care our friend needs but inwardly—I hate to admit it—shuddering. We asked what the average age of the residents was. Eighty-five, we were told. Many of them seemed to be just sagging into old age. If life treats me unkindly I may be one of those some day, I know, but I'm not ready yet to be part of as elderly a community as that.

When I mentioned this to Luverne, he remarked that Pilgrim Place's policy of not admitting residents over 75 provides for a younger, livelier community. Interesting! He isn't discarding entirely the idea of moving there some day—perhaps?

The pain of letting go.
March 28

TODAY ONE OF LUVERNE'S FORMER STUDENTS now serving overseas spoke at the chapel service at the college. Last Sunday two of his former students, a gifted couple, were commissioned for missionary service. About fifty of Luverne's former students are in Christian ministry of some kind. He has found so much joy and satisfaction relating to his students; to quit teaching will be a wrenching, ripping experience for him. Can anything replace it?

Fear a prelude to courage?
March 30

OUR LAST WEEKLY chaplaincy training session tonight. To begin with, we talked a little more about the dying patient and grief and bereavement. Our lecturer's words activated scenes from the night my sister died making it difficult for me to pull back my traveling mind and focus it on the lecture. We took a short break. Contrary to custom I poured myself a cup of strong coffee. After reassembling, our chaplain gave us our certificates designating completion of the course, then proceeded to assign us to our floors. My name was next to the last to be called.

"Millie, your assignment will be ICU, CCU, and the neonatal ward."

I felt my mouth gap open. Had I heard correctly? I hadn't expected this! To be assigned to those floors! I was too dazed, too shocked to speak, to protest.

Our chaplain handed out the schedule for our continuing education meetings, our days of visitation, and then led us in closing prayer. I walked out, still reeling, into the moonless, clouded, cheerless night. At the corner, turning onto the main street, which seemed strangely deserted, I drove past darkened buildings. Only a 7-11 store offered light, but I saw no cars parked outside. At home, pressing the button to open the garage, I drove in. Slowly I pulled myself upstairs.

I was more scared than ever. I wanted to back out. I felt hopelessly inadequate. Perhaps, I thought, as I crawled into bed, perhaps tomorrow I should call the chaplain and tell him this assignment is too big for me.

I didn't phone him this morning. I am still scared, but in my heart I know I must at least give it a try. When I agreed to come to the training sessions, I did so only because I felt God was wanting to lead me out of myself and redirect my energies to caring about others. How then can I run away now?

The stairs to finding courage winds.
April 7

"I'LL BEGIN MY hospital visitation next week," I said to Sister Vicki this afternoon. We were sitting in the Quiet Room at the center, I at ease.

"Oh," said Sister Vicki. She looked at me intently. "Is your heart responding with joy?"

I hesitated, but I had learned I can't lie to Sister Vicki.

"I'm afraid."

"I can understand."

We sat in silence for a while. Then Sister Vicki spoke. "Millie," she said, "I think the time has come for you to practice a more disciplined prayer life."

"Oh," I said.

"Sunday afternoon I shall be meeting with two others who will begin the discipline of prayer drawn up centuries ago by Ignatius of Loyola. I'll explain what it involves at that time. Can you come?"

My feeling of being at ease vanished immediately. For some reason I couldn't articulate, I sensed if I agreed, I would be placing myself under the searching and scouring, the scraping and carving of the Holy Spirit in a way I had not experienced before.

"Tell me a little more," I stalled.

"Come on Sunday and I'll tell you."

"How much time will it require?"

"Only an hour a day."

An hour a day! My uneasiness was increasing steadily. I opened my mouth to protest that I couldn't possibly find an hour a day to . . . I hesitated, I couldn't say I couldn't find an hour a day to pray —what would Sister Vicki think?—but before I could say anything, Sister Vicki said, smiling, "I'll be expecting you at three o'clock."

What could I say? I had asked Sister Vicki to be my spiritual director until I could find my way out of the confusing world into which I have been thrust. I shall have to go, but I am feeling as apprehensive about this as I do about beginning the chaplaincy visitation.

It's all right to be afraid.
April 10

THE FAITHFULNESS OF GOD in meeting my needs never ceases to impress and amaze me. Has it been merely by chance that I have been reading Madeline L'Engle's book *A Wrinkle in Time* at this particular time? Last night I came to the part where Little Meg was speaking to herself as she was seeking courage to resist the strange pulsing evil force of IT, the Evil One who sows seeds of doubt and unbelief. Little Meg says to herself: "Father said it was all right to be afraid. He said to go ahead and be afraid. And Mrs. Who said—I don't understand what she said, but I think it was meant to make me not hate being only me, and being the way I am. And Mrs. Whatsit said to remember that she loves me. That's what I have to think about."

So it's all right for me to be afraid as I face my chaplaincy work, as I begin my Ignatian studies? All I need to remember is that Jesus loves me. What a relief!

And then an added word came in my devotional reading for tonight from Charles de Foucauld where he reminds me that "Our Lord is on our side, with us, upholding us."

So I turn again to our Book of Worship and reshaping one of the prayers a little I pray: "Lord God, you call me to ventures of which I cannot see the ending, by paths as yet untrodden, through perils unknown. Give me faith to go out with good courage, not knowing where I go, but only that your hand is leading me and your love supporting me; through Jesus Christ our Lord. Into your hands I commend my spirit. Amen."

All beginnings are somewhat strange.
April 15

I MET TODAY ALONG WITH TWO OTHERS, strangers to me, at the Center for Spiritual Development for the introductory session to the Ignatian studies. In spite of the comforting, reassuring words I had received from God, my uneasiness still persisted, and I had not been able to leave it at home. Sister Vicki picked it up and asked, "What is troubling you?"

I didn't answer. She looked intently at me, then said, "We'll work at this together."

She spoke first of preparation for prayer, of taking time to free our minds from wandering thoughts and harrying concerns that prevent us from hearing God speaking to us.

Then she explained to us that the Ignatian method of study is not meant to be a substitute for an analytical, intellectual investigation of the text. Both methods carry value, she emphasized, the one speaking to the heart, the other to the mind, but if you can integrate heart *and* mind, you will be able to draw even more abundant and sweeter waters from the well of the Word.

Most of the readings, I understand, will be scenes drawn from the

Old and New Testaments with occasional readings from one of the Old Testament prophets or one of the New Testament epistles. We are to read the passage several times, perhaps even several days in succession. She noted that as we do this we often will notice things we didn't when we read the text the first time. She explained that we are not to seek to squeeze as much meaning out of a portion as we can, but rather become aware of what is grabbing our attention and focus there.

She went on to explain that we are to use our imagination, putting ourselves into a scene and experiencing and living it. "Using your imagination will help you in learning to to meditate also," she promised.

As we enter the scene, she said, we may find ourselves identifying closely with a particular individual. For example, when Jesus is about to cross the Sea of Galilee, we may find ourselves balking at getting in the boat. Then we are to ask ourselves why; and only when we are ready to get into the boat will we be ready to move on to another story.

At the end of each exercise we are asked to pause and reflect, trying to identify where we were aware of the Holy Spirit stirring in our hearts. Sister Vicki suggested we write these responses in a journal.

All this sounded very mysterious to me, but I said nothing.

"After you have persisted in this study for several weeks," Sister Vicki continued, "review your journal. If you have noted certain feelings or responses frequently, for example, if you have recorded feeling confused, distracted, upset, depressed, at peace, released—any emotions that reoccur—look at the texts you studied. Ask if the responses rose out of the texts, if so, what texts, and what prompted the response. If not out of the text, ask if the emotions arose out of some concern of yours, some event, or how did they come into being?

"If you are willing to return to the places of discomfort," she said, "and stay there until you feel a new movement stirring in you, you will discover you are moving from anxiety to trust, from fear to hope, from darkness to light, from struggle to surrender."

I marveled that she was so confident that God would speak to us.

"Simply present yourself to him," she urged. "Fling open all the rooms of your heart so he may enter through his word which has transforming power. Through that Word he *will* affect, mold, and change you. The work is his and his alone; your work is to rest in him."

So I begin yet another new venture. Help me, God.

Face your fear and it will vanish.
April 20

I ARRIVED AT THE HOSPITAL TODAY early enough to pause first in the small chapel where no outside noise intrudes. Closing the door, I sat in silence. I felt inadequate, helpless, scared. I would have preferred staying home but had managed to get myself in the car and out of the garage.

I sat in the chapel telling God how frightened I was. I asked for help. I prayed for grace to leave my own cares and concerns in the room with my Lord when I left.

When my pulse slowed to normal, still praying, walking to the elevator, I rode it to third floor. At the end of the short hallway I gently pushed open the swinging doors that would admit me to the world where people confront death and eternity. Strangely enough, once I had passed through those doors I found myself relaxing. Even more strange, I felt I had come home.

At the nurses' station I checked the records, then walking to the first curtained-off cubicle, I slowly pushed aside the curtain a little, peeked in, introduced myself, and asked permission to enter.

In the first cubicle I found a radiant 86-year-old, his round, cherub-like face still rosy, his eyes spirit-alive, his hair an uncontrollable white mist.

"God has given the wife and me sixty wonderful years together," he said, gasping as he spoke, "and as if that wasn't enough, he let me do work I loved."

"What work gave you so much satisfaction and joy?" I asked.

"Paperhanging," he said. "Put that paper on the walls real careful-like, and when it is done, stand back and look at the room and see what a pretty scene you have created." He chuckled softly. "Of course, there were a few duds too—people who chose the wrong paper—at least

I thought it was wrong—some paper I used to really shake my head over, but I guess life's like that too, some happy things, some disappointments. Gotta focus on the beautiful ones; forget the duds."

I thought of John Coburn's statement a friend had included in a letter recently to the effect that we become joyous and thankful persons by constantly, consistently, day by day offering up prayers of thanksgiving. Our responses to God determine the kind of persons we become. "What kind of a person do you want to become?" Coburn had asked. "If a joyful person, then thank God."

How old was the next person I visited? Over 80, surely; I hadn't noticed the age on his chart.

"Only one child we have," he said, "but what a girl she is! When she got married we thought she had found a man who would love and provide for her, but instead, do you know what he did? After they had three small children, he walked out on her, then sold the house from under her and disappeared. She never got another penny from him. No child support, nothing."

"Well, the Mrs. and I, what were we to do?" he said. "We took them right into our home, and the Mrs. cared for the whole family including the little ones while our daughter and I worked. We raised those kids, yes, we did. And do you know what she, our daughter did? Last year when a stroke flattened the Mrs. and she lay all paralyzed, not able to talk or feed herself or nothing, that daughter of ours quit her job and cared for her mother a whole year until the Mrs. died. Now ain't that something?"

He stopped to brush away a tear, "I suspect she'll do the same for me too if I get out of this place and need her care."

The skin of the next man was badly jaundiced, his cheeks sucked in. He lay there dying because he never believed he was an alcoholic, never sought treatment and help. When I asked if I could enter his space, he shook his head in refusal and turned his face to the wall. Saddened, I left.

After completing all my visits on the ICU and CCU wards I took the elevator to the neonatal ward. I could do only one thing there. Going from incubator to incubator I laid hands on each incubator and prayed for each fragile life lying inside, their lives sustained only by tubes. I don't know how many of these children ever will be prayed for as they grow up, but I am determined that at least they shall be prayed for now.

One little one I prayed for has a mother who is a heroin addict. She gave birth to him after carrying him only twenty-six weeks, but because of the technological assistance available he lived. But what will the future hold for him? How much neurological damage has he sustained? His mother refuses to sign papers releasing him. Will she seek rehab, care for him properly?

The single mother of another preemie has AIDS. How long will the mother live? And after that, what? I came home from my first day of visitation both saddened and cheered.

> *O Joy that seekest me through pain,*
> *I cannot close my heart to thee;*
> *I trace the rainbow through the rain*
> *And feel the promise is not vain*
> *That morn shall tearless be.*
> —*George Matheson, 1842-1906*

Dancing with our shadows.
April 22

I'VE BEEN THINKING TONIGHT about the trip we took to Sequoia with Dave, Becky, and their little family a couple of years ago. We were cocooned together in a cabin and as daylight dimmed, we lit an oil lantern and hung it from a hook on the far side of the room. The lantern's flickering light cast mysterious shadows around the room, and little Rachel, standing on the bed, discovered an enlarged outline of a person etched on the opposite wall.

For a moment she just stood and stared, uncertain as to what she was seeing, a little afraid—perhaps? Then cautiously she lifted an arm, and the dark shadow, obeying her, lifted its arm. Her head she tipped, her leg she flung out, her body she bent. Whatever she did, the shadow did. Her fears vanished and, enchanted and delighted, she began to dance, giggling, chortling, and laughing, enjoying her shadow.

That night, as I was lying waiting for sleep to come, I thought I heard God's Spirit whisper softly, "We all have shadow sides, Millie. We don't want to own them. But if, trusting me, you will face your shadows, I will liberate you so you can discover a golden shadow hidden underneath and like your little grandchild, no longer afraid, dance with joy."

When we drove away from Sequoia a couple of days later, I left behind more ready to truly pray, "Search me, God, and know my heart." Why then, have I felt hesitation about following the Ignatian studies?

Choices made previously affect us in our later years.
April 27

1 FELT SO SAD TODAY because of what one aged man, sitting by the bedside of his comatose wife, told me.

"We both worked all our lives," he said. "Trouble was we spent it as soon as we earned it. Overspent too. Maxed all our credit cards, then couldn't pay the interest. Lost one house. A real nice one. Vegas got a lot of what we earned. Kept hoping we'd win the big one.

"All I have left now is a 50-year-old 800-square-foot house. Because my son is unemployed, and his daughter is divorced and with a kid, four generations of us live in that little house. But I need them to live there with me too, so I can pay taxes and fix things that go wrong, like the roof that I'll have to replace before the rains begin. When the wife and I got married we never thought life would end this way for us. Things sure ain't worked out."

Caring for God's abode.
April 30

OUR CHURCH GROUNDS are looking so nice. Some scraggly, overgrown bushes have been dug out. Others stand neatly trimmed. New shrubs have been planted. All the planters boast flowers in bloom.

"Our people have been busy," Pastor said. He named one of the retired men and added, "He plants and weeds the flowers. Spends hours here. Next week a team will begin giving some of the rooms fresh coats of paint. Thanks to . . ." and he named some, mostly women, "the workers always are well fed."

One has to choose in life.

May 4

ENJOYING A LEISURELY BREAKFAST this morning, Luverne and I talked about how five of our friends already have moved away, three have gone back to areas where they grew up, and two have built homes close to their children. Others haven't moved yet but have plans to move and are letting choice locations determine where they will go. We fantasized a bit about possibilities open to us.

"Imagine," I said, "year-round watching the sun set on the other side of a Minnesota lake. I could go for that. But I wouldn't like the mosquitoes," I quickly added. "Or humidity."

"Worse, the cold winters," Luverne said. "How'd we get along after all our years in tropical or warm climates?"

"But our extended families live there," I said. "And Janet and Ron. And most of our old-time friends and retired colleagues from Tanzania days."

"I know," Luverne said slowly, "that appeals." And then he added, "But why not stay on right here, where we are? What's wrong with that?"

The phone rang, and that's as far as we got with our conversation.

Wise words about decision-making.

May 13

PAGING THROUGH A MAGAZINE TODAY I came upon an article that quoted the advice Luther had given when people had asked if they should flee the bubonic plague or remain where they were. Luther suggested they consider a few questions as they made their decision.

- Will the action I'm considering hurt others?
- Does it fail to do the duties of my position as a neighbor, a child, a parent, an employee, a citizen, a shopkeeper, a public servant?
- Can I do what I'm thinking about without injury to the love I owe my neighbor?
- Do my action and attitude flow from trust in God's care or from my fear?
- Can I do this without disobeying God's commandments?
- Does this action foolishly threaten me and my well-being without serving others?

As long as people could answer those questions with integrity and with love for their neighbor, Luther said they could consider any choice "right." But what if they still were in doubt as to what to do? In that case, Luther said, study the scriptures, pray, talk to other believers who can become the voice of God to you. Review your life history, your past experiences. God is always present to guide us in our decisions, Luther declared. If we don't have that guidance, it may be either because we haven't asked for it or don't want it! Search me, God.

Considering carefully all the options.
June 9

BECAUSE WE'RE TRYING to consider carefully different possibilities open to us, we spent the day looking at smaller houses as a realtor drove us around, but we came home shaking our heads. None we had seen "clicked" with us.

Tonight, as we sat out on our patio eating supper, Luverne said unexpectedly, "I've been thinking that I don't want to own a house anymore."

I stopped eating, my fork mid-air, and looked closely at him.

"Tired of caring for one?"

"Wouldn't mind giving it up."

Well! This is the first time I've heard this from him. So what do we do then? Rent? Where? And what?

Narrowing the options assists decision-making.
June 18

THIS EVENING AS WE WERE EATING SUPPER again on our patio I asked Luverne if we could discuss the kind of home we would like to live in the rest of our lives. We agreed we both wanted a place on one floor—no more stair-climbing. We each want a study of our own. We want two bathrooms. We also want to live close to a church and good medical facilities.

"Where will we put the children when they come to visit?" I asked. "And the grandkids."

We weren't sure how to answer that. How big a house did we want?

And then I asked if I could tell him what I really want. Luverne looked surprised and said, of course. I really want to be in or near a facility that offers, if and when we need it, extended care—care with meals, laundry, housekeeping, etc. I said. I told him I'm tired of moving, that I don't want to move some place now and then move again. And for the hundredth time I repeated that I didn't want our children to have to worry about what they were going to do with old Mom and Dad when they need extended care.

"They already have enough, what with caring for their growing families," I said. "I don't want to add to their loads."

Luverne sat silent for what seemed to me like a long time. Finally he said, and I think he found it difficult to get out, "If all this is a 'must' for you, then we better consider a retirement community."

Then he suggested that we visit some. Whoops! It was my turn to draw back.

I said if we want one in this area I didn't think we needed to visit any; we pretty well knew what they offered. And I think we're too young for the ones we know about, I said. He agreed.

They don't offer the space we need either, I said.

He mentioned some large retirement communities that offer space. I knew what he was referring to. Yes, but, I countered, many, perhaps most of the people living there spend their time in leisure activities. Would we be happy in that environment? And besides, if you need nursing care, you have to move out.

We picked up the dishes to carry inside. In the family room Luverne switched on the evening news, and after the broadcast somehow we didn't pick up the conversation again.

The essence of a trusting relationship.
June 20

1 CONTINUE MY WEEKLY VISITS with Sister Vicki. She is praying with us that God will give us wisdom to make the right decision. Her companionship on my journey means so much to me! I think of the words of George Eliot: "Oh, the comfort, the inexpressible comfort of feeling safe with a person, having neither to weigh nor measure words, but to pour them all out, just as they are, chaff and grain together, knowing that a faithful hand will take and sift them, keep what is worth and then, with the breath of kindness blow the rest away."

As Sister Vicki suggested, I have set aside a special journal for my Ignatian studies, and it is filling up. As I continue day by day I think I perceive a slow but gradual movement within me away from the tenseness and anxiety I knew at the beginning of the year to one of being more relaxed and trusting. But I still have a long way to go. When I get discouraged because I make such slow progress, I think of Arnold Bennett's words of counsel which I entered in my quotation book once: "Beware of undertaking too much at the start. Be content with quite a little. Allow for human nature, especially your own."

Tug-of-war.
June 22

A NEW DEVELOPMENT! A letter from Pilgrim Place came today about a builder/applicant program. Six duplexes will be built on undeveloped property. Builder/applicants will pay for the buildings, then live in them at a substantially reduced fee or rent. The investment in the building also will be deducted from the builders' assets when the builders pay a percentage of their assets as an entrance fee.

One attractive feature of this plan is extended residency of fifteen years in the home for a surviving spouse. Ordinarily at Pilgrim Place if a spouse dies, the surviving spouse is required to move within six months to a smaller home, usually one with only one bedroom, a living room which varies in size, a bathroom, and a small kitchen. Some of these homes are quite comfortable, though small, but a number are tiny.

Each of the duplexes to be built will enclose 1,330 feet, accommodating two bedrooms, a small study, two bathrooms, a combination living room and dining room, and a kitchen with a small breakfast nook. We could convert the second bedroom to a study. David went with us tonight to look at the site. We walked around it, talked; and before we left Pilgrim Place, slipped into the mail slot of the administration building a check, a deposit as requested, to indicate our interest. However, by making a deposit we are not signing a contract. We still can withdraw our offer, so I continue to be torn by conflict. I agonize. If we decide to become builder/applicants, we will be making a sizable investment. If we live long enough, we will come out all right financially. If we don't, our children will be the ones who will feel the loss. They have chosen service professions paying modest salaries. Any financial assets we can leave them will be of immense help. At the same time, we would be making the decision largely to relieve them of the responsibility and anxiety of caring for us.

My feelings are mixed up too because I sense that Luverne is taking this first step, not because he would choose it for himself but because he wants to do this for my sake. I am deeply grateful; he loves me dearly, I know, but I want him to be happy too.

At the same time, I am worried. Will he be happy there? I'm almost sure he would prefer "living on our own" and possibly in a rural area. I also am confused because it appears that Luverne and I have switched roles in making this decision. I have viewed myself as the risk-taker and Luverne the conservative decision-maker. In this instance, Luverne would be willing to continue living on our own, trusting (risking?) that God will care for us in one way or another. I, who have considered myself the risk-taker, now find I want the security of a place where we shall be cared for regardless what happens.

I am confused also because I have argued for my preference almost entirely from a rational point of view. In the past, I have made decisions governed by both reason *and* feeling. This time I have let reason control me. This new person I have discovered within me surprises and even frightens me a little. I wonder what has occasioned the change. Will I discover myself changing in other quite radical ways also? Who is this new person I am living with?

Does Luverne have any regrets about taking the first step we have? If he has, he hasn't said anything.

The fact that the duplexes won't be ready for occupancy for at least another year or more eases some of the tension. Also the letter is being sent to twenty potential builders. If more than six apply, lots will be drawn. Can I not trust God that if we are not to make the move, more than six will apply, and in the final drawing our name will be eliminated? I need to place this matter in God's hands and leave it there.

Disturbed.

June 28

THE DYING SUN, slanting its rays as it hit the calloused desert floor, exposed its cracks and wrinkles.

"Looks like the tough, leathery hide of an old bull elephant," I think. But I know the desert floor's tough appearance is only a mask, for the crust, in reality, is as fragile as an eggshell, easily fractured, broken.

The taut skin of the old man lying on his bed in the hospital was leathery and gray, his hands, though bony now, roughened and toughened. His voice, was gruff, his words few, his manner disturbed.

I sat quietly by his bed, then cautiously rested my arm on his bed. He moved his scrawny hand close to mine, laced our fingers together, and then he spoke. The gruffness, I was about to learn, was only a mask.

"I wonder," he said, "what my report card will look like when the Great Teacher hands it to me."

For my dying friend the *presence* of God more profoundly disturbed than his absence.

Another step forward.
July 29

𝒜 LETTER FROM PILGRIM PLACE informed us today that six couples have applied to build, so now they will be able to proceed with building plans. If more apply before the cutoff date, lots will be drawn; so a measure of uncertainty continues.

Stories worth broadcasting.
July 30

INSTEAD OF ALL THE STORIES of hatred, violence, beatings, murder, and rape that the TV portrays night after night, why don't they tell stories of love and kindness? During the years we lived in Singapore, the TV there did just that. I could have put broadcasters here in touch with a worthwhile story to tell today.

She lay comatose, a shrunken old woman, the veins on her skeletal arms purple and bulging, her skin spotted where blood has leaked out under the skin, her head swollen from a massive brain hemorrhage. A slender, long-haired young woman sitting by her side was holding her hand and weeping silently.

"Mother?" I asked.

She shook her head.

"Grandmother?"

She shook her head again.

A nurse came in. I stepped out. Evidently noting my puzzled expression, another nurse said, "There are three more of them in the lounge."

Who were the "them"? I found them sprawled in chairs, dozing.

"Is she the mother of one of you?" I asked.

"No, just a neighbor," a young man spoke up. "We're college students. She has been living in the little house her husband built when they got married but squeezed in now between apartments where we live."

"She's such a sweet little old lady," another said. "Lives alone now. She'd bake brownies for us and invite us in . . ."

"And strawberry pie in the strawberry season," the youth added.

"We wanted to thank her," the first one spoke up again. "So we started taking her grocery shopping, driving her to the doctor, mowing her lawn; it's been such a privilege to be able to do something for her."

"She's been like a mother away from mother for us," the third one said.

I wanted to hug all of them.

But my heart ached a few minutes later when a man in his early forties, dying of AIDS, told me to get out, he didn't want to talk to anybody.

Renewal in planned idleness.

August 10

Hᴏᴍᴇ ꜰʀᴏᴍ ᴀ ʀᴇꜰʀᴇꜱʜɪɴɢ, renewing interlude. En route to Judy's for a visit we spent the night at Kingsburg. In the evening we sat under the stars in a park and enjoyed an old-fashioned band concert. The people who attended had dressed up for the event!

Judy treated us to a dinner at a French restaurant. Gourmet food. Mmm! Then Judy, little Alison, and I attended a play about Cinderella. Alison stood up throughout the play, watching and listening intently. As we walked out, I said to her, "Not all our dreams will come true, Alison, but we must never stop dreaming." She looked up at me with her trusting blue eyes and smiled.

En route home we drove through Sonora Pass. Saw jillions of tiny mountain flowers. Aspens whispered. Lodgepole pine sighed. We spent the night at June Lake, nestled among the Sierras, relished fresh trout at the Sierra Inn, relaxed in the pool, strolled through the village. As daylight faded, we sat on the porch outside our motel room listening to the owls and the water of the lake gently slapping the beach below. At midnight a crash, bang lightning and thunder storm put on a wondrous display for us followed by pelting rain driving against our window panes. How we Californians love rain! And finally we wound our way home through the Mojave Desert and the Angeles Forest.

Thank you, God, for Luverne, who understands my need to unwind and plans so many enjoyable trips to help me find renewal in idleness.

A woman of faith and vision.

August 24

1 VISITED AN AGED WOMAN TODAY, her white, silk bedjacket trimmed in lace accentuating her fragility. Frail and dainty she looked, frail and delicate as a butterfly, her skin parchment-thin, but her age-blue eyes were twinkling impishly.

"You have children living nearby?" I asked.

"Six sons living with me," she said, "at least I call them my sons."

Further conversation revealed they are young men recovering from addictions to either drugs or alcohol.

"How fortunate they are to have you!" I finally managed to say.

"No, no," she protested, "you don't understand. I am the fortunate one! They visit me every night. Last night when the pain was quite dreadful, one of them held me in his arms and sang to me until I fell asleep."

The direction set.

September 13

1 RIPPED OPEN THE LETTER from Pilgrim Place this morning and read that only six have applied to build the duplexes, and we are one of the six. So we're "in."

Ambivalent feelings still play around within me.

How will I fit in living with graduates of Yale, Harvard, Princeton, and other prestigious colleges and universities, I who have not enjoyed the privileges they have?

Most residents voice their pride in being liberals. I'm more conservative than liberal—not conservative as some think of as conservative, but conservative in my theology. My faith belief means a great deal to me. I don't want it belittled.

I support the need for social action and justice and believe my life will be enriched by those who fervently work for it, but I hope some gatherings will offer me something with which I can nourish my soul. Surely that will be provided also. Can't imagine it not being a major emphasis, especially because we are elders. And I'm not a committee person, and I dislike immensely being constantly busy doing, doing, doing. Residents have assured me I can choose to be as involved as I wish. At the same time I know friendships develop as people work together. I know also that the community places high value on those who participate in their activities and especially in the festival. I can understand this also because this builds community, but at the same time I hope there will be a small nook left for quiet people. However, I know I need to move beyond thinking of my own wants and desires and ask instead what I shall be able to bring to the community. I shall need to find places where I can use the gifts and strengths I do have.

I need also to stop thinking of those in the community with whom I probably shall differ not as "they," but "we."

As to the duplex itself, I couldn't call it our dream house. We'll be squeezed into a corner with a cement block wall separating us from our neighbors on the north and west sides with only seven, eight feet between the house and the wall. Our lawn in front will be the size of a postage stamp. Most difficult for me to make peace with is that when we sit in our breakfast nook we shall be looking through the patio door at our neighbor's storage shed. Yuck! I would have liked more storage space also and a garage, and I shall miss our spacious patio area. We'll have to guard against accumulating things, which in itself can be good.

The duplexes won't be ready for occupancy until a year from October at the earliest so that gives us another full year to enjoy this home, which I intend to do.

Year Three

Building Faith;
Unbuilding
a Home

The call.
January 27

THE PHONE RINGING AND RINGING this morning pulled me from deep sleep to consciousness. In the dark my hand searched for the phone, found it, dropped it. I stroked the carpet. Couldn't locate it. Staggered out of bed, flicked on a light switch, retrieved the phone.

"Yes? Hello. Hello!"

"I . . . can't . . . breathe! I'm . . . afraid. Come."

Who on earth? Janet? Calling from St. Paul? What time is it? Janet? Let me talk to Ron. . . . Janet's still sick? Yes, yes, I know you phoned a few days ago. . . . Yes, yes, I remember the breathing and swallowing problems. . . . But you said the doctor wasn't worried. . . . He kept Janet overnight in the hospital? Told her the next morning it was psychological? . . . To go back to work? . . . And she's worse now? . . . Another doctor thinks maybe it's MS?! O, no! . . . Janet wants me to come? . . . Ron, how? This is winter. Minnesota's icy roads. I've never driven on ice. Had I told you that Dad's due for hernia surgery too? . . . Yes, again. I can't leave him . . . You have to keep up with classes at the seminary? . . . Yes, yes, I understand that. Janet's afraid to stay alone? . . . Says it's terrible when she can't breathe. Yes, yes, I know. Oh, Ron, give us time to think; we'll call back."

Sleep had fled. Slipping on robes and slippers, padding downstairs and filling mugs with milk, we waited for the milk to get warm. Then encircling the mugs in our hands, we talked. An hour later we called Ron, asking if Janet could come here. We'd pay for her ticket and take care of her here.

The icy grip of fear.
January 30

JANET CAME TODAY, Ron's mother accompanying her. When I saw the airline stewardess wheeling Janet down the ramp in a wheelchair, I grabbed the railing. I hadn't expected this! The saliva was drooling out her mouth; she clutched a small towel under her chin to catch it.

Her face, usually rosy with health, was wan and bleached of color; her cheeks sucked in.

"You've lost weight!"

"Twenty pounds." I scarcely could decipher the words.

"I didn't know you were this sick!"

At home we immediately phoned the neurosurgeon for whom Janet had worked summers, and who had become like a friend to her and described her condition to him.

"I'll call right back," he said.

He did. "Listen carefully," he said. "I've made appointments with an internist, an ENT doctor, and a neurologist. Jot down who, when, and where. They'll see Janet immediately."

Summoned to trust.

February 13

THE DAYS HAVE DIFFUSED one into another. As we have consulted the various doctors, we've listened with fright to possible diagnoses.

"Lupus, maybe," one said.

"Could be multiple sclerosis," said another.

"Meningitis?" questioned another.

Other unpalatable suggestions have been made. Stroke? Virus-caused paralysis?

At home Janet has been struggling to swallow liquids. Sometimes she succeeds; sometimes it comes out through her nose. Spasms of coughing rack her being.

Anxieties regarding the future exhaust both Janet and us. She has spent years training to be a pastor. Will she be able to speak intelligibly again? The speech therapist she is going to will give no promise. Janet loves her work. The thought of giving it up devastates her.

In order to assist Ron with his seminary training, she has been serving in a church. If she can't continue working, how will Ron be able to complete his training? If Janet is not able to work again, will they be able to live on one salary? Have a family?

"You won't die; you will recover," the doctors say, "but it will take months."

"Completely? Will I be able to work again?"

The doctors fall silent. We are indebted to them for the way they have given of their time, even coming in on days off, but we yearn to hear words of promise and assurance.

"If we could have seen you at the outset, we could have done some tests that might have helped us diagnose your disease," they say.

But we can't relive those days. Instead we have to ask, How do we go on from here?

Helplessness.
February 14

$\mathcal{T}$HIS IS A BAD, BAD TIME FOR US. There is no way I can begin to understand what Janet is experiencing, to be unable to swallow, to have deep coughing rack, convulse, and weaken my whole being, to hear only slurred, garbled words come out when she tries to speak.

I can't understand, but I am her mother who loves her dearly. I ache with that love. I hurt immeasurably because she is suffering so intensely. I long to cradle her in my arms, to protect her, to comfort her, to make her well. But I cannot.

I sense the loneliness she feels. Her breathing these days, because of anxiety, too often runs at too swift a pace. When fear builds to an unbearable pitch, she erupts, pushing me away. I understand, but still it hurts.

Our worlds have become porcelain ones, shattered, splintered with pain. Even the weight of air seems too heavy to bear. She whom I love, my child, I wish to be free from anxiety, from illness, from fear, and instead to be well, to be whole and at peace again; but I lack the power to heal her. I am helpless. I can stand by her, but the battle, in one sense, is hers. She will have to find her own way through; I cannot do it for her.

The comfort little children offer.
February 16

WE BURIED ANOTHER OF OUR FRIENDS TODAY, one of our peers. Luverne couldn't attend; I had taken him to the hospital early in the morning for hernia surgery. A friend offered to stay with Janet while I was gone.

Becky, David and the children came just before I left for church, so after the funeral I picked up Chinese food and brought it home. Depositing my parcels in the kitchen, I carried our mail upstairs to my study and quickly leafed through it: an invitation to lead a retreat, write an article for a periodical and speak at a convention. I wondered if life will ever allow me time and energy to resume these activities. I stood gazing out the window and then I thought, but I'm not the only old parent who sometimes wonders when concerns for adult children will end. This morning I had snatched a few moments for a quick walk and on the way met a neighbor who wanted to talk.

"What shall we do?" he asked. "We have one daughter who doesn't want to do anything else but pray. A thirty-two-year-old son is living at home—says he is too stressed out and worried about the future to work. And on top of all this, my mother-in-law is seriously ill."

The voices and laughter of the grandchildren downstairs floated up. Leaving my mail on the desk and hurrying downstairs, scooping them up and hugging them, I felt their soft kisses on my cheek. And then for the next few hours, putting aside my anxieties over Janet, choosing not to expend energy even in hoping, and determining not to live with my eye on the morrow, instead I sought to absorb the intrinsic value those hours of reprieve offered me, meriting celebration.

"Look at the birds of the air!"
February 19

"WE ARE THE PEOPLE OF HIS PASTURE," we sang today as we knelt at the communion rail. I thought of how my father always carefully saw to it that our cattle had enough fodder to eat. The year of the drought he rented additional pasture land.

I turn to the sixth chapter of Matthew and try to hear Jesus speaking to me: "Look at the birds of the air; they neither sow nor reap nor gather into the barns, and yet your heavenly Father feeds them. Are you not (are Janet and Ron not) of more value than they? So do not worry about tomorrow, for tomorrow will bring worries of its own. Today's trouble is enough for today" *(Matthew 6:26,34)*.

Can I *really* hear Jesus speaking to me? What expression is on his face as he says these words? Where are we? I want to spend time placing myself in this scene. . . . Half an hour has passed. My heart is leaping in joyful response. David of old and I are singing together:

> *On the day I called, you answered me,*
> *   you increased my strength of soul.*
> *You stretch out your right hand,*
> *   and your right hand delivers me.*
> *The Lord will fulfill his purpose for me;*
> *   your steadfast love, O Lord, endures forever.*
> *Do not forsake the work of your hands.*
> *(Psalm 138:3,8, NRSV)*

Why pray?
February 25

TODAY FAMILY MEMBERS and a few friends gathered for a healing service for Janet. Tonight as I sit alone here in my study I ask myself what meaning does prayer for healing carry if no healing takes place. Why pray?

This question has taunted me ever since we prayed that our second baby would live and he died. I think I've made peace with the unanswered question; and then a new situation arises, and the question sticks its sneaky head up again, sneering at me. It's been happening all afternoon, clouding over my hope.

Then tonight, sorting through some of my files, I came upon an issue of the little leaflet "Context." Betty and Art Winter had interviewed Monsignor Geno Baroni, former Assistant Secretary in the U.S. Department of Housing and Urban Development, and a Catholic priest, who at age 53 was dying. Winters asked Baroni how he prayed. Baroni replied that he asked Jesus to come with him, that his body, a temple of the Spirit, is hurting. He tells Jesus he is hurting, that he hopes in him, but he isn't sure what he is supposed to do. Fight back? He asks for grace to put his suffering in the context of a day-to-day testing.

Winter asked Baroni if he had experienced healing after prayer.

Baroni replied that some days he did experience calmness and peace, and then the fear would leave. But, he added quickly, it wasn't like that all the time.

Winter then asked him how prayer helps him then if it doesn't bring healing.

Baroni had thought for a while and then said that prayer brings him into God's presence. He tries to remind himself of the promise, the victory, the hope, the resurrection. And he tries to see this present situation as merely a temporary one.

He told Winter he would urge people who are sick to get someone to pray with them. Henri Nouwen had been coming every other day and praying with him, he said.

Winter wanted to know what he did at night.

Baroni said he simply prayed, "Okay, Jesus, I surrender. Help me. I'm in your hands. Take care of me. Amen."

I drew both help and comfort from Baroni's words.

Visualizing healing.
March 5

$\mathcal{T}$ONIGHT'S READING yielded another encouraging word to follow Baroni's simple words of counsel. This time it was some words of George Stewart which I remembered having read before but needed to focus on again. "No situation remains the same when prayer is made about it," Stewart insisted. "For a time things may seem to go on much as before, but the decisive power has entered in, and even mountains must move. Prayer always creates a new situation."

In my mind's eye I return again and again to the scene of our service of healing for Janet and imagine the life of the resurrected Christ pouring into her, and then I follow that by visualizing her whole, well and healthy again.

The meaning of love.
March 12

$\mathcal{A}$LMOST SIX WEEKS HAVE PASSED since Janet came to us. She is still losing weight, but the loss has slowed down. Janet's suffering rips at my heart. Now that the nerves are coming back to life, her tongue sometimes chases uncontrollably all around inside her mouth for hours. Her chin will tremble, her vocal cords will twitch, and sometimes the entire upper portion of her body will shake convulsively. I try to prop pillows around her in bed, but it does no good. I watch helpless.

When the sheer torture caused by these uncontrollable nerves peaks to heights seemingly impossible to bear any longer, she vents her frustration, fear, and anxiety. She needs to do this—the only problem is sometimes I get in the path of the venting. I have marveled at her stamina, her powers to endure. I know I probably would not have been able to bear as much as she has; but because my relationship to her as her mother is so intimate, I cannot be an objective caregiver. She *is* bone of my bone and flesh of my flesh.

The pain that sears me because she suffers burns white hot; and thus, struggling with my own anguish, I sometimes do not respond to her appropriately. I seek to comfort, forgetting, as Daniel J. Simundson counsels in *Faith under Fire*, that "the question is when to say words of hope and when to delay it, because the lament has not run its course." Because Janet is still lamenting deeply and thus because I am unable to comfort her, I feel utterly helpless. This only increases my pain.

Sometimes, secretly I resent this child of mine. Irrationally, I feel like screaming at her, "Why are you so sick? If you weren't so sick, you wouldn't be causing me so much pain!" and these thoughts trouble me most of all.

I was crying tonight when Judy called.

"I shouldn't feel this way, Judy," I sobbed.

"Mother," she said, "you don't expect to have the same feelings of love toward your children all the time, do you? Love means not giving up on them, not disowning them, not necessarily feeling loving toward them constantly. Loving is caring for Janet, and that's what Dad and you are doing."

Later this evening I picked up L'Engle's book, *A Circle of Quiet*—I guess I was wishing I could find a circle of quiet into which I could crawl for a while. Anyway, was it mere chance that I came upon a quote she had included by Edward Nason West in regard to *agape*, the Greek word for love? West had noted that love means "a profound concern for the welfare of another without any desire to control that other, to be thanked by the other, or to enjoy the process."

These days are so hard for all of us, dear Jesus. It's like being thrown into a stormy ocean, inundated, coming up, gasping for air, only to go down again.

Love never ends.
March 13

$\mathcal{A}$FTER JANET'S STORM HAS SUBSIDED, she always comes to me.

"I'm so sorry I'm behaving as I am these days. I don't know why I am. I wish I didn't."

She allows me then to hold her, to dry the tears on her cheeks.

How true that the flame of love will not go out. It may smolder and smoke, but then whoosh! A few words spoken, a kiss pressed against the cheek, a tear, and the smoldering coals spark to blaze again.

The ability to be truly loving people
*   is the greatest gift of all.*
It is that gift which most of us appear to possess
*   in such small measure.*
We talk a good deal about it;
*   we make grand statements concerning it,*
But when the chips are down, we usually find our
*   vaunted love in short supply.*
The true lovers are the people who are empowered
*   and motivated by the love of God.*
Theirs is a selfless, truth-seeking, all-enduring love.
They love in the measure that they acknowledge
*   and experience God's love for them.*
They discover that their response to divine love
*   must be demonstrated*
*   in their relationship to humanity about them.*
Love, authentic love, is eternal
*   and propagates and perpetuates love.*
The ability to love is truly the supreme gift—
*   the gift to which we all should aspire.*
*   —Selected portions from "1 Corinthians 13"*
*   Epistles Now by Leslie F. Brandt*

A time to remember and give thanks.

March 15

WHAT KIND OF A FOLLOWER OF CHRIST AM I? What kind of a mother am I?

Janet survived; she could have died. Her speech is improving daily; she could have been left with an impediment. She is able to swallow better; the doctors appear confident she will continue to improve. Her congregation most generously has offered to make up the difference between what her salary would have been and what her disability check will give her; if they had not, Ron and Janet would have had to borrow money so Ron could complete the school year. They have medical bills to pay; the bills could have been much greater.

I have so much for which to be thankful, so how did I spend the morning? Fretting and grumbling inwardly, because housework and caring for Janet and her needs takes so much time my writing assignments lie uncompleted on my desk. Ever since I began to write I've lived with this tension, between my wanting to write and the demands being a parent places upon me.

But why do I chafe because I have a family? If I had not had a family I would not have known Luverne's love all these years, been encouraged and enabled by him to write. When I've been gone leading retreats or speaking, he has scrubbed floors, cooked meals, and done the laundry. I never would have dared undertake our two overseas journalistic trips without him to help me in making arrangements and traveling with me as well as shooting photographs to illustrate my articles. No, unquestionably, without Luverne I wouldn't be where I am today as a writer.

And if I had not had a family, I would not have been able to watch four choice individuals develop, each in his or her own way, children to take pride in, who comfort and support me and generously express their love and appreciation. And now our family circle is widening to include spouses and grandchildren who delight, amuse, and cheer me up.

Why, then, do I ever find it difficult to celebrate parenthood? Is it because our culture's strong emphasis on the individual versus the community erodes my sense of values?

My lot is not heavy, O God. Because of accidents, disease, or divorce that their children have suffered, many parents my age carry much heavier loads. O God, you, who in your word describe your love and concern for us as both mother and father love, you understand us and regard us with compassion. Give, not just to me, but to all parents who become weary in their roles, the love, patience, understanding, and strength we need to carry on.

Dare to dream.
March 19

ONE OF THE DOCTORS said to Janet regarding my belief that she will regain her voice fully, "Your mother is a dreamer."

I'm not sure I understand what he meant by that, but I know I must hold fast to dreams, for if dreams die, as Langston Hughes once wrote, "life becomes a broken-winged bird that cannot fly." I need to remember this also in relation to my desire to become a better writer.

Late evening

MY BIBLE READING FOR TONIGHT contained this verse from Psalm 131:

> *But I have stilled and quieted my soul*
> *like a weaned child with its mother,*
> *like a weaned child is my soul within me.*
> *(Psalm 131:2)*

I am grateful, God, I can nestle down in your arms tonight and be at rest.

Why not laugh?
March 20

INCIDENTS THAT ORDINARILY I might even be able to laugh at upset me these days.

I came home from the supermarket this afternoon carrying two full bags of groceries. Because my stiff, arthritic knees sometimes cause me not to lift my feet as high as I should, I tripped on the curb and landed flat on top of eggs and bread.

Luverne came running.

"Are you hurt?" His forehead was all wrinkled like it gets.

I shook my head, tears not allowing me to talk.

"Then why are you crying?"

"I'm mad because I'm getting old!"

That struck him funny. He threw back his head and laughed, and then I too began to laugh.

Love bytes from God.
March 21

HOW GRATEFUL I'VE BEEN for visits from David, Becky, and the grandchildren, telephone conversations with Judy, friends, and my extended family, and weekly sessions with Sister Vicki.

Sister Vicki has been a tower of strength for both Janet and me, taking us by the hand and leading us to Jesus so we can lean on his arm, and then anchoring us to him so we can find solid footing for our feet again. When doubts that Janet will recover completely enough to resume her calling as a pastor have stifled hope, rendering me unable to pray, Sister Vicki has slipped an arm around me.

"You're tired, Millie," she says. "I'll do the praying for you. You just rest."

She has given Janet a ceramic piece of two hands, cupped open.

"Imagine yourself as resting in the hands of Jesus," she has said. "Let him hold you."

I continue with my Ignatian studies because I know that now more than ever I need to trim the wick of the lamp that burns in this temple, to add more oil, and to turn the flame a little higher so the light can burn a bit brighter. But my hands tremble, and so I cannot trim the wick evenly; and this causes the flame to smoke, and I sometimes spill the oil also when I try to pour it into the lamp.

"You're trying too hard," Sister Vicki says. "Trust God to take care of both Janet and you."

But moments of grace also come, and to Janet too: a verse of scripture or a song speaks to her; sometimes a sense of God's presence and peace suffuses her entire being with warmth. These experiences she finds profoundly and deeply healing.

When I was a child in Minnesota and zero-degree weather had ceased weaving laces on the window panes because warmer weather was moving in, and when the birds began to trill the songs of returning spring, I sometimes would find my way to the creek that ran through our farm. There, kneeling in the thinning snow and putting my ear down close to the ice, I would listen carefully. If I could hear the faint trickle of water running underneath, all glory would build up in me. Soon all the ice will melt, I would think. The water in the creek will run, and I will be able to sail my paper and wooden boats down the stream again. What expectation, what joy coursed through me as I knelt there, the wet snow soaking my long socks and winter underwear. Now again, I think I hear the water under the ice flowing. Soon that water will run free again, I tell myself, and Janet will be completely well.

Hope surges to the surface.
March 30

JANET'S CONTAGIOUS GIGGLE and the impish glint in her eye are reappearing. She can swallow soft food now.

Good-byes are always hard.
April 2

WE SAW JANET OFF AT THE AIRPORT yesterday bound for her home and Ron. It was dreadfully hard parting with her, but our love and prayers go with her. Her doctors here have advised her to get in contact with a doctor as soon as she returns.

Families working together.
April 12

RON'S FATHER has been taking time off from work many days to drive Janet to Mayo. There he has waited patiently while a team of doctors examine her and her records and take certain tests. They finally have reached a consensus on diagnosis: Guillain-Barré syndrome, a virus-borne disease that paralyzes.

In a few rare cases it may paralyze the entire body permanently; more often recovery follows after extended rest, and in some instances the case may be so light the patient recovers rapidly. In certain cases, however, the disease leaves some residual effects.

Usually it presents itself from the feet upwards. In Janet's case it began at the top of her head, paralyzing speech and swallowing and making breathing difficult. This unusual presentation had caused confusion for the doctor who saw her after the onslaught, and thus he had ordered no spinal tap, which would have identified the ailment.

"You are extremely fortunate to be alive," one of the doctors said to her. "Of those affected in breathing as you were, and who are not put on a respirator immediately, a high percentage die." And then he added, "You are a very strong person and basically very healthy. I am sure you are going to continue to recover steadily."

However, he cautioned her that a year and a half of rest might be necessary. Her congregation, declaring that they didn't want to lose her, graciously had extended her leave of absence until September; but Janet will not be able to return to them in September. However, with Ron doing his internship next year, they will manage financially.

"I know. I lived through it."
April 26

1 PHONED THE REFERENCE DESK of our library today and inquired if they could help us locate a support group for those recovering from Guillain-Barré syndrome. A woman called back later and gave me the name of a woman in Pennsylvania and her phone number. I called her. She proved to be the wife of a surgeon who had suffered from the disease and recovered, though not sufficiently to continue his practice as a surgeon.

She asked where Janet lives, said they had a friend there, another doctor, who also had been struck down with Guillain-Barré. She asked for Janet's phone number, called their doctor friend, told him about Janet, and gave him her phone number. The doctor called Janet immediately.

"When can you come and see me so we can talk?" he asked.

Janet called after they had met. "Mom, it was wonderful!" she enthused. "We talked and talked. He knew just how I've felt, and he could explain so many things."

I hear the ice over my little creek breaking up, and through the cracks and crevasses I can see the water flowing.

> *Bless our God, O peoples,*
>   *let the sound of his praise be heard,*
> *who has kept us among the living,*
>   *and has not let our feet slip.*
> *For you, O God, have tested us,*
>   *you have tried us as silver is tried.*
> *We went through fire and through water;*
>   *yet you have brought us out to a spacious place.*
>   *(Psalm 66:8-10,12)*

Our Vietnamese memorial wall.
May 7

THIS MORNING AS WE DROVE through the iron gates of Queen's Park Cemetery, I could feel my heartbeat quickening. An anniversary celebration of the church Luverne had served for ten years had brought us to Calgary a few days ago. Today we had our own private and special event to observe.

Thirty-five years ago we had buried our second little son next to his little brother who had died a year earlier. At the time the officials of the cemetery had ruled against markers or monuments for the graves of babies; but a few months ago when we had made the request again, they had relented. From our home in California we had ordered the marker, engraved with the names of our two sons, their dates of birth and death, our names as parents, and to link them with us, the site where we hope one day our bodies will lie. A niece who lives in Calgary had overseen the installation of the marker. When we received news from her that the marker was in place and that our former parish would be celebrating an anniversary in May, we knew the time had come for a pilgrimage back to Calgary.

We had little trouble finding the site; Luverne remembered it well. The ground was still moist with morning dew. What did it matter? I dropped to a sitting position. With the palm of my hand I wiped away the moisture from the marker. The granite felt cold under my touch. Then with my forefinger I traced the names of our two little boys. Momentarily I got lost wondering, as from time to time I have wondered, if they had lived, what would they have looked like? What kind of personalities would they have had? What professions or callings would they be pursuing now?

As I sat there, tears flowed freely. I know the tears will never cease, but the tears, while they remain tears of loss, are no longer tears of bitterness, but of gratitude, not of doubt and unbelief, but of trust and faith.

During the many long years that have intervened, I have been learning, little by little, and oh! with so much faltering, slipping, and falling, to turn over my stubborn, independent, willful spirit to God. I have learned the value of owning my emotions and acknowledging them openly at least to God and myself. I also actively have sought understanding and help from God's word, from those trained in the nuances, responses, and reactions of the emotional and psychological side of our beings, seeking to become willing to listen to God and others, to be corrected and repent, and to be humble and teachable. As I have worked at learning these responses, in both joyous and sorrowful experiences of life, I have been able to hear God wooing, counseling, and schooling me to live with life's unanswered questions—though it seems as though the schooling is a never-ending process!

Unanswered questions, sweeping in their breadth and stupefying in their complexity, present themselves to me more frequently than ever, but I think I now am learning to leave these with God—at least most of the time. I am grateful I can do this and acknowledge that God is God.

How long I sat there this morning I do not know. I was faintly conscious of the wind ruffling my hair, the sun gently warming me, and a bird occasionally breaking the silence with song.

"Shall we go, Honey?" Luverne's soft-spoken words finally interrupted my thoughts.

The dew around me had evaporated; only the grass under me was still damp. The marker under my hand was dry and warm, and when I drew my hand away, I noticed the beams of the sun dancing and playing on the dark granite surface.

"Well?" Luverne's voice again.

I reached over to pet the names on the marker one last time, then lifted my face to his and extended my arms. He pulled me to my feet. I stood for a moment, holding his hand, my eyes moist, my heart full, and my spirit at peace.

A surprise announcement.
June 3

"*I* THINK WE SHOULD put the house on the market to sell," Luverne said as I handed him his tea this morning. I was so surprised I almost poured my tea on my Total instead of in my cup.

Why did his announcement unsettle me? I knew if we were going to move we would have to sell the house, didn't I?

Lonely but flying.
June 7

*T*WO LETTERS CAME TODAY. One was from friends who had volunteered to go for a short term to an overseas position. They found themselves in an isolated area. They had returned home now after having completed their assignment.

"We were lonely and terribly homesick," the woman wrote.

The other letter was from a 90-year-old friend who, in his first two lines, wrote of his hope for a soon reunion with his "pal of almost a lifetime"—his wife. Then he used the next three-fourths of the letter letting words spill out as he enumerated all the blessings he was enjoying living in his "cozy, memory-filled apartment" in a retirement complex, with an optional dining room—"to supplement my skill with microwave and can opener"—a health clinic, exercise room, bank, offices, small grocery, and pharmacy in the complex. He wrote about living close to family and "my beloved church." He was enjoying studying the Bible with a group and regular meetings with a men's group.

At the end of his letter he called attention to his coat of arms printed at the top of the page. A shield, slashed in two, enclosed in its first half a cross set in a circle. In the second half of the shield sat a bumblebee.

"As you may know," he wrote, "according to the law of aerodynamics that clumsy bug can't fly. But because he doesn't know it he just flies anyway." He then compared himself to that bee who not knowing he is unable to fly still continues to "fly."

He longs for a reunion with his "pal of almost a lifetime," but he isn't waiting to "fly" until then. Cheers!

The unbuilding begins.

June 23

WE'VE BEGUN THE TASK of preparing the house for sale. Luverne spent the week hauling out all the lumber from under the house and giving it away, painting the trellis over the patio, trimming the bushes and fertilizing the orange and lemon trees.

I laid new bedding plants in the earth.

Nostalgia.

June 30

SPENT ALL WEEK cleaning out the garage. What nostalgia! Broken bats and split whiffle balls, baseball gloves of all sizes, worn-out footballs, beachballs, volleyballs, golf balls, eighteen tennis balls, a broken tennis racket, an odd ping-pong paddle, a small boy's T-shirt.

What busy youth our children were! And now gone are those days. Aging brings sadness.

'Tis the gift to be simple.

July 13

DAY AFTER DAY the unbuilding has gone on. A realtor told me a house elegant in its simplicity attracts buyers, so we've told the children to come and haul away any furniture we won't take with us that they can use. Tomorrow I'll drive to a friend's home who is having a garage sale and learn from her how to set one up.

Persisting in the discipline of prayer.

July 26

HELD OUR FIRST GARAGE SALE the 20th and 21st. People arrived early. Some cruised around, scanned, and appraised like experienced buyers. Some bought; some didn't.

Then from the 22nd through the 25th I took time out to attend and teach at a writers' conference. Over 200 present.

We took time out to attend two weddings also. I savored all the joyous celebration.

I've also continued filling my journal for my Ignatian studies with my questions and reflections. Spending an hour a day in meditation and prayer—there have been days when I haven't been able to give that much time to it—has helped me get through all the past months have brought us. I question that I would ever have persisted in this discipline if I hadn't been meeting with Sister Vicki regularly and making myself accountable to her.

Care, repair, and maintenance.

July 27

WASHED THE WOODWORK and all the light fixtures today. Some days ago we selected and ordered new carpeting and padding for the entire house. The men will come tomorrow to lay it and also will put new floor covering in the bathrooms and kitchen. Luverne called a roofing company today to come and check the roof.

Tired.

August 4

I'M SO TIRED I don't want to wiggle a toe! Washed all the curtains and sent out the draperies to be cleaned. I've replaced the draperies in a couple of the rooms but didn't spend a lot of money on the new ones. How do I know what the next owners will want?

God's mysterious moves.

August 8

I'VE BEEN THINKING about how when we move I'll have to discontinue my hospital visitation. The thought saddens me. Then today I received a phone call from an editor at Abbey Press asking if I would accept an assignment to write a *Care Note* on "Letting Tears Bring Healing and Renewal." He explained that *Care Notes* are colorful, attractively set-up, eight-page pamphlets to be used by individuals, churches, hospitals, or care centers.

I'm delighted with this opportunity, enabling me, in one sense, to continue my chaplaincy ministry. And surprised by God! He didn't even give me a chance to ask him for something to take the place of my visitation. (I'm smiling.)

Joy and pain.

August 10

*Y*ESTERDAY AT THE HOSPITAL I prayed with a Muslim. At first I hesitated to ask him if I could pray, but he said, "Yes, yes!" so quickly, I felt at ease. At the end I saw his eyes damp with tears. He joined the palms of his two hands together and prayed.

I joined the palms of my hands together. "Peace be with you," I responded.

He was too ill for further conversation, so putting him in God's hands, I left him.

In the neonatal ward on the charts in the space for religion, all the parents had written, "None."

I found a wee one born the day before yesterday lying with her pencil-thin leg in splints, her leg broken because her mother, an unmarried woman, had given birth to her in a toilet and tried to flush her down.

I had trouble sleeping last night after that visit.

The unbuilding ends.
August 13

FINAL TRIPS TO THE THRIFT SHOP for Luverne today. The garage stands empty now except for the cars. A friend will store and use our tent trailer until Judy can pull it to their new home in northern California. With their recent move farther north, Barry and she and the children now will be a two-day trip away from us.

No longer home.
August 17

WITH THE ACTUAL DATE for listing the house scheduled for tomorrow, I cleared the top of the kitchen cupboards today, tucking all the canisters, the mixer, and the toaster behind closed cupboard doors. Instead I've placed a lush green plant and an African violet in one corner. The cupboards inside, if anyone opens them, stand uncluttered and beautifully in order also.

In the other rooms I've packed away all photographs and personal mementos. A bowl of dried spices makes fragrant the fireplace nook.

For Open House days I'll arrange fresh flowers to place throughout the house, have a CD ready to play and turn on all the lights.

This afternoon Luverne and I walked around the grounds and garden and then through the house. What we saw pleased, we agreed. But, I said sadly, it's no longer our family home. Instead it's just a house ready to go on the market.

Go on the market. As soon as the words escaped from my lips I felt them hanging in the air like winter's icicles. I shuddered. But if moving away from, moving toward—goodness knows, what—meant putting it on the market, our family home . . .

Luverne must have picked up my feelings, because he asked if I would like to go out for dinner. We went but neither of us was hungry, and it wasn't any easier when we came back either.

Choose the direction you want to look.

August 18

THIS MORNING I LOOKED DOWN from my study and watched a realtor pound a "FOR SALE" sign in the newly mown lawn outside our house. I turned away suddenly, swallowed hard, and then resolutely sat down to begin working on my first *Care Note* which I am writing for Abbey Press's *Care Notes* series.

I am so pleased with the attractive, eye-catching format of these helpful little brochures that are placed in hospitals, care centers, and churches. What a privilege to be writing some of them!

With joy I think about this, my first assignment, "Letting Tears Bring Healing and Renewal." Am I crazy writing about joy and tears in the same sentence? I *am* full of joy that I can write. I *am* full of joy that in writing about the healing and renewal that can result from crying I can see the redemptive nature of all the tears I've shed the past years.

What do I want to tell my readers? I want to tell them that looking through tears during the weeks surrounding my husband's cancer surgery changed me. It helped me cherish my dear ones more every day, to long to know God better, and to watch for God in the commonplace events of life. I understand better now what is really of consequence. My life has become richer and more focused.

And while every testing, every loss, every crisis is an invitation to move on to a new life, courage is needed if we are to respond affirmatively. But the tears that spring from our love can help us find healing and renewal. And with healing comes new courage, enabling us to say,

"I am determined to honor myself and those I love by moving on and living! God is with me! I shall trust and not be afraid!"

Displaced for a day.
August 20

YESTERDAY, OPEN HOUSE DAY, we moved out, displaced persons, homeless for the day, but it was better that way. Better that we not see those for whom the sign had gone up, for whom the unbuilding had been done.

The need to say good-bye and let go.
August 23

TODAY AS I WALKED in the ICU ward I saw a Hispanic woman crouched in a corner, her fear and bewilderment clearly evident. She had smoothly combed her long black hair and was wearing a freshly washed and neatly ironed dress and apron.

One of the nurses told me they finally had been able to locate Ruperto's mother living in Mexico. She speaks no English.

Ruperto is the young man who has been lying in the last cubicle for weeks. His "friends" dumped him off, drunk and stoned, at the emergency door one night. Then driving off and calling from a pay phone they asked the hospital attendants to look outside the door. No identification was found on the body. Somehow, I don't know how, police came up with a name and began the search for his mother.

Ruperto's brain is dead, but he had signed no Durable Power of Attorney statement, probably didn't know one existed. Spanish-speaking nurses and social workers have talked with his mother; but when they bring up the subject of removing life-support, she tears at her hair, rocks back and forth, moans and shakes her head in protest. And so Ruperto continues to lie there, looking like an ivory waxen figure with tubes going in and out, machines keeping his heart beating and performing the functions of his organs. It's so sad. I wonder what dreams that Hispanic mother had for her son when she used to hold him in her arms, feel his searching lips connect with her nipple and then listen to his murmurs of contentment and baby joy. And how sad to see a young life that could have been bursting with promise wasted.

O compassionate God, cradle that frightened, grieving mother in your arms. Help her to let go.

Healing is a continuing process.
September 6

CONNIE, ONE OF OUR VOLUNTEERS who is also a nurse, asked me today how it was going for me to visit the neonatal ward. I told her I wouldn't have missed the experience for anything.

Connie's remembering that night at our chaplaincy training, I thought, touched by her thoughtfulness, the night I had broken down when the psychologist had spoken about the supreme importance that parents be given the opportunity to see and hold their babies if they die. I had been denied that privilege with our two little ones.

"A measure of healing on a deeper level is coming," I said to Connie. "Looking at those wee premature babies, I am better able to visualize our little ones. Because I wasn't allowed to see them I've always wondered how they looked. Also I've learned how, even if preemies survive, their future sometimes remains uncertain. Some continue to have chronic problems. I wouldn't have desired that for any of our children." I hesitated. "Or for me as a parent. I don't know how able I would be to care for a disabled or developmentally impaired child."

I waited a while and then I added that life is a mystery, and I face many questions in life for which I can find no answers. We had two other children who were born prematurely and survived, and that had happened in Africa in a seven-bed hospital with no technological provisions to care for them—not even an incubator or oxygen. And today we couldn't find two healthier children.

"No, Connie," I said, "I don't have the answers to many of my questions; but as I've grown older, more and more I have come to believe that more important than receiving answers is to be able to respond in a redemptive way."

Questions God asks us.

September 13

THIS WEEK I MET a Turkish man who spoke no English, and a Romanian who told me that when he got out of the hospital the first thing he wanted to do was find a church home. He had been baptized in 1978 in Romania, and had recently come to the U.S. Then he proceeded to tell me part of his life story, filled with tragedy in so many ways.

A Jain, a Buddhist, two Muslims, a Hispanic, and a European immigrant. I've visited all of them the last weeks. At an unprecedented rate our country, our states, and our communities are heaving with change, as we evolve into a nation of many nations and many religions.

Vietnamese are erecting an impressive, ornate Buddhist temple immediately across from our church. "FOR SALE" signs are going up in many places as former owners move away.

What will this movement, both coming in and leaving, mean for our congregation, for the people who have formed intimate, supportive friendships in our congregation? Having seen what has happened in so many places, I can't help asking these questions. How many will be afraid to talk with, listen to, and learn to know those of another culture, another religion? How many will simply flee? Again and again I hear God calling us to move into a new now. How we shall respond remains for each of us to choose.

Lord of all nations, grant me grace
To love all people, ev'ry race;
And in each person may I see
My kindred, loved, redeemed by thee.
  —Olive Wise Spannaus

Useless fears.
September 20

SOMETIMES, LIKE TODAY, my friends in the hospital with whom I have visited do not speak of God helping them. He is, I am sure, but they have no awareness of it. Today only one troubled soul opened up and spoke about his distress, his fear of death.

I wonder how it will be for me when my time comes. Will I be consciously aware of God's help? He has promised he will never, never leave me nor forsake me, but ... I remember the godly man who cried out in agony as he lay dying because he said God had disappeared, gone into hiding; he couldn't feel his presence.
That's hard both for the dying person and the family and friends standing by.

But I must not allow myself to focus on this! Instead I must say to myself over and over, "Whether I am conscious or not of his presence, God *will* be with me. I can depend on him. All will be well."

Knowing also that the suffering ones in my hospital and all the other hospitals and even care centers represent only a minority of the aged who suffer like these do helps also. Many, many aged ones do die suddenly, in their sleep or peacefully at home.

I must let the unknown be just that, the unknown. I act foolishly if I add to my uneasiness about the unknown, fear. And since I do not know what may lie ahead, why shouldn't I begin to live seeing possibilities in the aging years, seeing them as liberating, not restricting, beneficial, not harmful, capable of producing personal growth, not limiting or destroying it?

Gratitude and Swiss cheese.
October 11

A YEAR AND A HALF have passed since I began my chaplaincy visitation. As I have listened to how my friends planned or didn't plan for the future, they have instructed me. As I have observed the way in which they now bear their pain and suffering, I have gained fuller understanding of how attitudes formed throughout life either support or weaken one in times of desperate need. As I have noted the ones who are blessed with friends or family who keep vigil with them, and as I have ached for those who lie alone, unvisited, uncared about, I have said to myself I must never forget the importance of reaching out in love to others, for without love all of us lose hope and give up.

I clasp to my heart and cherish the uncomplaining courage, genuine gratefulness, buoyant humor, and calm acceptance of what has happened to them that so many have exemplified. When tremors of anxiety and fear begin to ripple over me, I recall my friends and let their examples lived out for me alleviate my fears. If they, now so frail, so helpless, many of them knowing they will not return home again, have found the courage, faith, and strength needed to face death with noble dignity, then surely I shall be able to do so also when my time comes.

Thus the very chaplaincy visitation I had greatly feared has instead alleviated my fears and gifted me with renewed faith and hope in God. I've received far more than any small morsel of comfort, encouragement, or hope I may have been able to extend. God knew what he was doing when he prompted the chaplain to call me.

And now at our next chaplaincy extended training session I shall have to tell our chaplain of our anticipated move and with it my inability to continue volunteering here. Sadness creeps over me as I think about it. As I say good-bye to the suffering friends I've met week by week another hole will be carved out in my heart. I'm beginning to feel like a slice of Swiss cheese.

Waiting.

November 15

We wait and wait. Prospective buyers come and go. How often we've heard the words "We wish we could afford it," uttered, the yearning of those who speak deeply evident. We too wish they could afford it. They walk softly and quietly through the house. They speak softly and quietly.

I am weary of dusting every day, weeding, washing windows, always on the ready for the unexpected visitor to come, look, admire, and leave. In a few months we shall have to leave; our new dwelling place will be ready. Though not finished completely yet, we already have been told we can measure for and order draperies and blinds.

Finding a way out of gridlock.
November 27

LUVERNE, AWARE OF HOW DIFFICULT I am finding it to wait for the house to sell, has suggested we move small articles of furniture that fit in a friend's van and our car: dishes, pots and pans, linens, photographs, paintings, leaving only the necessities here.

A home can help define who we are as persons, so in choosing what to bring with us into our new home I'm trying to choose objects that do just that. Some of our furniture, however, is too large to fit into our smaller home. This we shall have to replace with other furniture, new or used. We also will not have room for many of our paintings and artifacts from different countries. Some of these we'll pass on to our children so that through these objects they can connect with their childhoods spent overseas.

In thinking of our new home I ask myself, "What do I want our new home to say?" I answer by saying that I want the objects we bring with us to connect us with our past, a past that played a significant part in shaping who we are as persons now. The familiar objects which we no longer shall see because we don't have room for them here or because we've given them to our children will signify in a symbolic way a departure and separation. We have left our past behind. What remains of our past is what has been integrated into our selves and the memories we have of the past.

But we are moving into a new now. I want to symbolize that transition also, but I'm not sure how to do it. The furniture we shall have to buy to fit into a smaller home will be one indication. Because it is smaller in size it speaks its own language, telling me that in our aging years we learn to downsize.

I also would like to add to our furnishings some art objects that Pilgrims at Pilgrim Place have created. Adding these would be, for me, a way of symbolizing our entry into a new community. As time goes on I'm sure I'll see other ways of portraying the transition from the old to the new that we are making. I view the decorating and furnishing of our new home as a creative venture.

The moving begins.
December 3

𝒟AY BY DAY we've been moving. We purchased bookshelves, and we've moved books, box after box of books, even though Luverne has had to part with the majority of his books.

We have moved enough now so the days we are working in our new house, we can pause at noon, take a break from unpacking, and prepare a simple lunch. A few of our neighbors have moved into their duplexes. Others will move in soon. Our duplex will be the last one to be fully completed. The administration at Pilgrim Place has been most understanding also as to our position in regard to selling the house.

Christmas with a daughter.
December 12

ℳINOR SURGERY FOR LUVERNE needed again, but we can wait until January. On December 23 we'll fly away to Minneapolis for Christmas.

But in the interval we shall welcome forty-one guests into our home: our church friends, the Chaplain associates, Dave's family, some visiting Norwegians, and six Japanese. I'm glad my little prayer remains taped on the fridge door, reminding me to Whom I turn for all the strength I need.

Thanks to God for my Redeemer,
Thanks for all Thou dost provide!
Thanks for times now but a memory,
Thanks for Jesus by my side!
Thanks for pleasant, balmy springtime,
Thanks for dark and dreary fall!
Thanks for tears by now forgotten,
Thanks for peace within my soul!

Thanks for prayers that Thou hast answered,
Thanks for what Thou dost deny!
Thanks for storms that I have weathered,
Thanks for all Thou dost supply!
Thanks for pain and thanks for pleasure,
Thanks for comfort in despair!
Thanks for grace that none can measure,
Thanks for love beyond compare.

Thanks for roses by the wayside,
Thanks for thorns their stems contain!
Thanks for home and thanks for fireside,
Thanks for hope, that sweet refrain!
Thanks for joy and thanks for sorrow,
Thanks for heav'nly peace with Thee!
Thanks for hope in the tomorrow,
Thanks thru all eternity!
　　　　　—August Ludwig Storm

Year Four

Part One:

Forging
a New Life

Part Two:

Anchoring in God

PART ONE:
FORGING A NEW LIFE

Witnessing the faithfulness of God.

February 1

FINALLY, FINALLY THE HOUSE IS SOLD, and as Luverne said would happen, to the right people and at a price fair and agreeable to all of us.

Friends told us to call the family. "They're moving to town; they'll need a house," they urged.

When I called, the man asked me to describe it and then said they would come and see it.

They stepped inside. Their glance took in the entry hall, the spacious living room and family room, the cozy fireplace nook, the three-level stairway leading upstairs, the banistered upstairs hallway overlooking the living room below and leading to our two studies. They noted the vaulted ceiling, the hardwood floors, the extra-wide patio doors, the patio, the garden visible beyond, the spacious kitchen.

"We love it!" they said.

God-honoring people they are. Prayer, love, and joy will continue to flow through our home. It is good, Lord, it is good.

P.S. God. Did you keep us waiting all these months so these people could get the house?

Departing.

March 1

THE BIG MOVING VAN PULLED UP in front of the house. We had moved so much earlier that the movers, young and strong, soon emptied the rooms.

"You go ahead with David to meet the van when it arrives," Luverne said to me. "I'll take a final look around and follow."

"You drive, Dave," I said. I did not trust my vision.

I got in the car and shut the door. We pulled away from the curb and drove off down the street. I did not look back.

Our new home, late evening

THE MOVING VAN lumbered in shortly after David and I did. The movers quickly and expertly carried in the rugs and furniture and placed them in position and left us to unpack the boxes. We hugged David good-bye, watched him drive off, then turning, walked back to our new little home.

Sadness, relief, questioning, anticipation, dejection, expectation— a sea of emotions swept over me. What we were giving up was clearer to me than what we were gaining. I knew this was probably even truer for Luverne than for me and wished I could do something to ease his pain.

As we were finishing our small, silent supper the phone rang. One of our closest neighbors inquired if we could come for a visit. When we stepped inside their home, all our other neighbors who are living in the other five Cambridge Way duplexes greeted us. "Welcome to Cambridge Way!" they chorused.

Thus the eleven of us are bonding together as we share mutual concerns and converse with each other. And tonight as we laughed together, my loneliness also vanished.

Adjusting to a new daily routine.
March 2

THE WALK AT NOON TO ABERNETHY, the dining hall, takes five minutes. As we walked, disquieting thoughts walked with me: would I like the food, eating with strangers day after day; having my workday split in two at noon?

We rounded a curve and my eyes saw canes, walkers, and wheel-chairs. A "beep beep!" moved us to the side of the road, and an electric cart sped by with a red flag flying gaily from the rear. I forced myself to look again, and this time I saw a younger-appearing woman run down the steps of her house and walk quickly down the road. Others also were walking at a good clip. I wondered briefly why the canes, walkers, and wheelchairs had filled my picture at first.

Spotting a woman with a statuesque carriage, involuntarily I pulled in my diaphragm and straightened; but at the same time, once again, I found my eyes would not let me ignore the bent-over bodies, the feet shuffling close to the ground, the hesitant steps. And now I am one of these, I thought. Oh, well.

Outside the building I saw displayed on tables lemons, oranges, kumquats, a few bunches of carrots, a couple of heads of cabbage, half a dozen small grapefruit.

One of our neighbors had caught up with us.

"Fred harvests the fruit from trees that have been planted and sells them," he explained. "The money goes into the residents' health-care fund. He plants a huge garden too. I expect the vegetables came from his garden."

I looked at the tall man behind the table impeccably dressed in a black suit, white shirt, and black bow tie. He doesn't look like a farmer, I thought.

Had my neighbor read my thoughts? "Fred was a missionary profes-sor in Brazil before he came here," he said.

On one of the tables inside the dining room, we found the papers designating the number of the table to which the computer had as-signed us for the day. Table 26. Weaving our way past tables and people chatting with one another, we finally located our table. I saw a group around a grand piano in the lounge singing lustily.

A bell called for everybody to be seated; someone, stepping to a microphone, led in table grace.

A stack of plates stood in front of one man, and after we had fin-ished eating our salad and the waitresses had brought the entrée and placed it in front of him, he began to serve.

"You missed the fish yesterday," one said jokingly. "We get fish every Friday."

"And pie every Thursday," said another.

"Roast of some kind, mashed potatoes, and ice cream on Sunday," the server said. They all laughed. Well, I thought, at least some things in my new life will be predictable.

Then the questions began. From where had we come? What work had we done previously? How had we learned about Pilgrim Place?

We dutifully answered the questions, then asked the other four at our table the same questions. As we conversed we learned one had lived at Pilgrim Place for thirteen years, another for eight, and two, who were our neighbors, had come in November.

I asked if they had known other pilgrims when they came. One said she had known at least twenty, another a dozen, yet another said he'd never counted, maybe two dozen.

"You know quite a few?" The question was directed to us.

"No, two. By name only. That's all."

An awkward silence followed, then the conversation veered off to topics of common interest to the others at our table.

"Coffee?" asked one of the women seated behind the coffee carafe. "Hot water?"

I allowed my attention to wander, and I glanced around the room. A sea of white and graying heads met my gaze. I sucked in my breath. Is this what I want? I asked myself. To spend the rest of my life looking at gray heads?

It is evening now. Our first full day here has come to an end. I sit in my study thinking and trying to process my thoughts, my reactions.

One thing is clear. Living here I cannot sidestep, deny, or fool myself into thinking I am not aging. If I try to, it will be like trying to escape from a lion and running into a bear. I sigh and wonder how difficult the process of accepting aging will be. How long may I expect it to take? Will I have to make peace with it before I can move on to search for and find a niche to fill in the years ahead? And then I pray.

Pursuing hobbies in retirement.

March 8

I OPENED THE DOOR THIS MORNING to find a distinguished gentleman standing outside. He looks like Colonel Sanders the Second, I thought.

"I've brought you a little present," he said, holding out a jar of honey. "My own."

"Your own?"

"Tending bees has been my hobby for 76 years," he explained. "Started when I was twelve. The custodian of our church died, and his wife asked if I would take care of the twenty-five swarms he left. I said, sure, not knowing what I was getting into.

"But twenty-five swarms were too many. I discovered the bees were managing me; I wasn't managing them. So I settled for three hives, then two, and finally one. Last year we had a bad winter, and I wasn't feeling well and didn't get over to the lemon grove to check on them. When I got there, I discovered the queen had died and with her the other bees. This is one of the last jars of my honey, but I want to give it to you. Beekeeping was a good hobby," he said, "one that I could continue even after retiring." As I watched him, cane in hand, walk away, I wondered if his hobby had contributed to the happiness he radiated.

Converting negatives into positives.

March 9

*A*T NOON TODAY a petite gentlewoman with a soft Southern accent sat at table with us. She was 96, she said. Her husband had died two years ago. They had been married over 70 years.

I said that after living together all those years losing a spouse must have been like losing part of yourself.

She agreed but quickly added that she didn't let herself think about that. Instead, she said, she thinks how wonderful they could spend so many years together.

I inquired how death had come for her dear one.

"A stroke," she said. "One to begin with, then later more. A year between the first and the last."

"Such a long time."

"Yes, but I was glad it wasn't longer. Only at the end was he completely paralyzed."

I asked where she lived.

"After my husband died I had to move. Now I live in one room."

"Every move is a loss."

"Maybe. But I get all my meals now. I don't have to cook. Someone cleans my room and does my laundry. I like that."

As we walked home together I asked her about her family. She had children?

"Yes, and I'm proud of them all." She paused. "Sometimes when I'm tempted to feel I'm good for nothing anymore, I look at them." She laughed. "At least I had something to do with producing them," she said, winking at me.

We had reached her door. Almost regretfully I said good-bye.

As I walked home I cheered in my heart this plucky little lady for her nimbleness in converting every negative into a positive. Undoubtedly, I thought, she's been practicing this for years, practicing it so long and faithfully that now the response is as natural to her as breathing.

The morning had been gray, dismal, and depressing, but now the sun was beginning to break through. As I stood watching the sun winning over the gloom I thought, I can't go back and relive the years that are past, but I can begin now to practice looking consciously but faithfully for the rays of the sun penetrating through cracks in the clouds that I may perceive darkening my entry into my new life here and now. If I forget to do this, will you please nudge me into remembering, dear God? Thanks.

Synchronizing two lives after retirement.
March 13

1 AM TROUBLED. Luverne too often sits silent throughout mealtimes. As I walk past his study lined now with only an eighth of the books that previously were in his library, his desk half the size of his former one, I see him staring out the window. He shows no interest in planting our little garden space. The stepping stones we had planned to lay from the front to our kitchen door remain stacked in a pile.

"The past two years have been difficult for you," I said today as we walked to Abernethy. "Your surgery. I'm sure you miss your students. And teaching—you always loved it. Your former colleagues, your friends moving away, so many of our friends having died. Too much loss in too short a space." I paused and then added, "I'm sorry."

I extended my hand to him. He took it. I said no more.

But this evening I blurted out, "But you know as well as I, Honey, we're the only ones who can determine how we'll adjust; the only ones who can choose to be happy or not."

He said nothing.

"Aging and retirement take away part of our lives, but they also free us to choose the way we want to spend our time as opposed to having to follow routines and schedules."

"You still have your writing!" he flung at me.

I do. In respect to our careers, Luverne has experienced greater loss than I. I had spoken too quickly. I need to allow him space and time to work his way through this adjustment.

But even if I still can continue writing, that doesn't mean I haven't experienced some losses too—the past couple of years especially, I think defensively. And moving here calls for adjustments for me too.

But men and women differ, I remind myself. It's easier for me to identify and express the emotions I'm experiencing. Sometimes I think our culture so thoroughly has schooled men to tune out their feelings some no longer are aware of them.

"I don't know how I feel." I've heard men say this when questioned about their feelings after having suffered a traumatic loss. If we don't know what our problem is or where or why we hurt, how can we find the answer or get relief for the pain?

But why is it, I ask myself, that many men experience no hesitancy about going to great lengths enlarging on some minor physical discomfort—especially to their wives—but to talk about emotional pain makes them exceedingly uncomfortable?

Don't women talk less about headaches or being tired or having sore feet than men do? Don't they also find it easier to tell one or two other persons about any emotional fermentation going on within them? Talking acts like a Pepto-Bismol for them, counteracting the acidity building up inside, bringing relief.

Maybe, I think, men differ from women also in that when something hits hard, they don't want to talk about it immediately. Maybe they feel a need to distance themselves from the loss first because they dislike speaking emotionally and want to recover sufficiently to speak more dispassionately and objectively. I really need to exercise more understanding, more patience, more sensitivity. Learn what to say to encourage Luverne to talk. Maybe allow him not to talk. Maybe just hug him more. Maybe that would be best.

However, as I reflect further on his retort, "You still have your writing," I wonder if I see in it his inference that my desire to continue writing restricts us from doing some of the things he'd like us to do together now. I guess there's truth in that. Having started to write so late in life, I don't want to quit writing, and that does limit our mobility to some extent.

I sigh inwardly. Here we are: two old people, one just over 70 and one approaching 70, still figuring out how to blend two lives because we each have some differing interests. Freedom always brings problems. In our case, it's the freedom that retirement from an employed position has brought Luverne and the freedom that the times have brought me, because women now can develop their own careers. I sigh again. Life never seems to get simpler. I think I better turn to my readings for tonight and then pray.

Acknowledging retirement losses.

March 14

WE WERE INVITED to a Pilgrim home after Vespers; and as we stepped inside, two other couples arrived.

After we had spent a few minutes in small talk connecting with each other, our hostess asked us what had been difficult for us after retirement or after coming to Pilgrim Place.

One of the men said he didn't miss the routine, schedule, and demands of the parish ministry, but he did miss the contacts he had with the people and also the pastors in the district.

One of the women who had been employed professionally missed her work. One couple lamented the distance separating them from their grandchildren and children, scattered over the U.S. "When we were busy at our work we didn't miss them as much; we more easily accepted the miles that separate."

One woman said she was missing her home state, the state of her childhood, and that she sometimes wished she could live there.

Listening to them I thought, I'm not the only one learning to adjust and took odd comfort in this realization.

Dealing positively with failed approximations.

March 18

FIVE YEARS HAVE PASSED since my last book was published, and I've written only short pieces in the interim. Life has been too disturbed, chaotic, and draining to concentrate enough to write. Now, as I try to recoup a writing schedule, I also find myself troubled by a sense of diminishment of time.

This morning I discovered my feelings articulated in *Aging: A Spiritual Journey*, where the author, Bianchi, writes: "Many creative writers have experienced a powerful sense of incompleteness in later life; they describe their work, as well as their lives, as 'failed approximations.'"

Elderhood can be a half-scared time, he noted, but added that "the most disturbing of times can become a season for innovative venture.

The very experience of 'failed approximations' can lead to new forms of reconciliation within the self." And then he pointed out that to learn humility, compassion, and care from our partially achieved strivings might be more important than to realize all our goals.

Accept limitations in good humor.
March 24

WE TALKED WITH A COUPLE TODAY, 90 and 92 years of age, who live in the assisted care unit. The man told how he had congestive heart failure five years ago; and afterwards, to begin with, the doctor wouldn't permit him even to make his bed. But gradually he improved, and one day he asked his doctor if he could make his bed again. The doctor said yes, just take it easy.

"The next morning the maid rapped on our door and asked if we wanted her to make the bed." he said. " I looked at it and said, 'Why not?'" He grinned. "She's been making it ever since."

I argue with myself on the way home. Maybe he's accepting the limitations of aging, but he's 92. I'm not 92 yet.

Feeling lonely.
March 26

1 WAS FEELING LONELY AGAIN TODAY, but reminded myself I've known times in the past when vagrant, troublesome feelings of loneliness have haunted me even when I've been at a party or have gathered for a family reunion. Sometimes, in fact, those occasions can be the loneliest.

However, I also know from experience I can do something about these feelings; and so today I picked up the phone and made three dates to meet friends for lunch or an evening meal. Before we moved here some of our friends had asked if they could come for a house-warming when we were settled. I called one of them today too and said, "Come! Please do!" So now we have four happy events to which we can look forward.

Basking in the warmth of hospitality.
March 29

*H*OME FROM ANOTHER DELIGHTFUL, relaxing evening in the homes of two neighbors. In the first home we sat and nibbled on hors d'oeuvres and chatted. Then we walked to the next home where steaming fifteen-bean soup, fruit salad, and fresh bread awaited us. Later, in front of a snap-crackle fire in the fireplace, we devoured homemade carrot cake and hot fudge sundaes with crème de menthe. We talked. We laughed. We shared stories. We came home happy. With so many people offering us warm hospitality, why do I ever feel unsettled, lonely, not at home yet?

Experiencing moments of unalloyed joy.
April 2

*T*HIS MORNING SITTING BY OUR KITCHEN TABLE rolling inch-size meatballs for our bean soup, I saw a flash of yellow streaking through the branches of the tree on the other side of the cement block wall separating us from our neighbor. A newcomer! What kind of bird was it? Then a bevy of blue jays, swallows, and wrens cruised in, flying in and out so recklessly among the branches and with such spirited abandon that the branches of the tree began to dip and swoop. Fascinated, I watched.

So absorbed did I become in their play that for a few short minutes I found myself forgetting my cares, my loneliness. I experienced moments of pure joy, and they brought to mind Robert Frost's verse, "A Prayer in Spring," wherein he prayed we might be able to enjoy the flowers and dwell in the springtime instead of moving into a harvest-time that was as yet uncertain.

Oh, give us pleasure in the flowers today;
And give us not to think so far away
As the uncertain harvest; keep us here
All simply in the springing of the year.

And make us happy in the darting bird
That suddenly above the bees is heard,
The meteor that thrusts in with needle bill,
And off a blossom in mid-air stands still.

Finding ways to feel at home.
April 3

"WHEN WE FIRST CAME, we found going away and coming back helped us feel at home," a Pilgrim said to me today when I was in the library scanning some books.

Once again I wondered what had prompted the remark, but I received the suggestion with a smile; and this afternoon I said impulsively to Luverne, "Let's go and see the grandkids."

So in the car we hopped and down the congested freeway we sped. An hour later we scarcely had pulled up to the curb before the children, who had spied us from the window, came tearing out of the house, arms flung wide to hug us, faces raised for kisses, shrieks and squeals of joy gladdening our hearts.

For the next couple hours, immersed in their jubilant enjoyment of life, all my feelings of loneliness vanished. Luverne was smiling and laughing, his old self. Things will work out eventually, I thought. We'll find our way through.

Fashioning a garden.
April 4

LUVERNE DUG THE STEPPING STONES into place today. Maybe we can begin work on our garden next.

Respecting the desire for privacy.
April 5

WHEN THE ELEVEN OF US MOVED into these six duplexes on this short "no through street" known as Cambridge Way, we truly formed an ecumenical community: two Episcopalians, two Methodists, two United Church of Christ, two claiming both UCC and Disciples of Christ membership, two Lutherans, and one Baptist.

Now Joseph, our Baptist neighbor, is ill. His cancer, which has been in remission, has reared its head. However, Joseph doesn't talk about it. Instead he continues to carry himself with the quiet dignity of the distinguished scholar he is, a winner of awards, and a former professor at the U of Iowa, the graduate school here at Claremont, and at Harvard. From acquaintances I've learned that he served as a missionary in Africa for four years and later lectured in numerous universities in Africa, the Middle East, and Athens. In our Pilgrim Place library I discovered two of his published volumes.

Joseph's wife died a year ago so Joseph lives alone now. We have noticed the little food car delivering noon meals to him, and of late he has looked so gaunt and wan Luverne and I are concerned. I had dropped a "we care" card in his box one day. He had not acknowledged it.

This morning I said to Luverne I wished we could help Joseph, but I didn't know what to do. Luverne suggested I ask him. I was slipping a note in his mailbox when the door opened unexpectedly. Although it was eleven o'clock Joseph stood there, clad in lounging robe, pajamas, and slippers.

"I'd prefer if you sent no cards or made no inquiries about my health or welfare," he said.

I stared and stepped back.

"I am a deeply spiritual man with adequate resources. I am at peace. This was true when my twenty-year-old son died and again a year ago when my wife died."

"I'm sorry," I stammered. "I didn't mean to intrude. I'm sorry if I've been clumsy in expressing concern. I just know how I've felt when the going gets rough."

"I'm all right, quite all right, understand?"

"You mean you want us to leave you alone?" Our eyes connected. We looked steadily at each other.

"Yes," he said.

I drew a long breath. "All right. I'll respect your wishes."

I took another step back. Joseph shut the door.

I couldn't help it. I felt rejected, rebuffed. However, tonight I've been thinking some more about it.

Unconsciously I have expected Joseph to have the same needs I experience in a similar situation. I had *wanted* him to have the same needs, because then I would know what to do to help him. I had forgotten the words of Friedrich Nietzsche: "The same passions in man and woman differ in temperament; hence man and woman do not cease misunderstanding one another."

If I am to really care about Joseph, I shall need to give him what *he* needs and wants, not what *I* think he needs or wants or what *I* want to give. The latter is merely selfish giving. But I can't give him what he wants if I don't know him, and I won't learn to know Joseph until he allows me to learn to know him. One thing is clear: he wants privacy. This we can grant him.

Gardening.
April 6

LUVERNE AND I WORKED in our little garden all morning. Our garden here is merely a narrow strip lying between the walkway and the cement block fence separating us from our neighbors on the north and west sides of our duplex, shady in some areas, exposed to sun in other areas, a difficult area to garden.

At noon we showered, changed clothes, walked to Abernethy and sat down at a table and were served. I counted it as pure luxury. At home after dinner, changing into work clothes, we worked some more, taking a coffee break in the afternoon. Only at nine o'clock did we sit down to enjoy our simple supper of sandwiches, vine-ripe cantaloupe, and ice-cold milk.

Later we looked at some slides of our family get-togethers. Then I luxuriated again, this time in a tub of bubbling hot water, soothing and relaxing for sore muscles and bones.

This morning, although I can see only the dirt under which lie the gladiola bulbs we planted yesterday and although the dozens of dwarf seedlings haven't grown a fraction, my mind's eye can visualize our little garden in full bloom, and I rejoice.

Reserving time for our loved ones.
April 8

ONE OF THE MEN WORKING in administration ate with us this noon. He told us his mother was 85. I said my mother died at 85. "More than a decade ago," I added. "Strange, but I think I've come to know Mother better since she died than before. I understand more and more what a remarkable woman she was."

"Why do you think this has happened?"

I had to think. "I'm older myself now," I said. "That helps. And when she died, she left a void. To fill that void I've recalled remarks she made and things she did. I also see now her mode of living and her decisions framed by the backdrop of her entire life. This has brought enlarged understanding of her.

"I only regret," I said, "that I didn't take time before she died to learn to know her better. If I had, I think we could have understood each other more sympathetically, cared for each other more sensitively, and supported each other more appreciatively."

"But you were busy with your own life."

"Busy, yes. And I took Mother for granted. She always had been there for me; I expected her to be always there . . . Strange, isn't it, how easy it is for us to deny the reality of death occurring to someone we love . . . or ourselves?"

Watching the train pull out.
April 13

‘LAST NIGHT sitting in the dimness of darkened Abernethy listening to the Pilgrim Place Ensemble play a concert in adjacent Decker Hall, unexpectedly the thought hit me with all the force of a strong jolt from an earthquake: "I'm here in this place *to stay*." Always before, I have anticipated another place to move to, another adventure to begin, but no more. This is the end of the line; the train won't go any farther.

Suddenly I wasn't sure I wanted to be here to stay. What had happened to me? Just a few months ago I had declared vociferously, "I don't want to move again—never!"

Receiving the gifts children offer us.
April 15

1 needed to get away, and so packing a few clothes we drove off to visit Judy and her family in northern California.

One day, five-year-old Alison and three-year-old Reed wanted to take Grandma and Grandpa for a walk in the Redwoods. I was not wearing walking shoes and my knees were hurting, but I determined not to say anything.

The path led us deeper and deeper into the woods until we came to an area with steps. My arthritic knees don't like steps. Carefully and awkwardly I let myself up and down the stairs. Little Reed, I noticed, was looking to the right and left of the path. Finally he darted off to one side and came back carrying a stout stick the right height to serve as a cane. This he handed me without a word. I accepted it with a smile.

When we came to the next descending stairs, Alison quickly stepped to my side and grasped my hand with her tiny hand to help me down the steps.

"You're just getting too old, Grandma," she said sadly.

"Oh, Alison, I'm not getting old," I said, "it's just my knees that are getting old."

She considered that, then asked, "Can just knees get old?"

Alison's favorite treat is doughnuts, so we always arrange for a visit to a doughnut shop where we sit at a table munching doughnuts together.

Time to leave for home came. Alison hugged me. "My favorite thing used to be doughnuts, Grandma," she said, "but now my very, very most favorite thing is having Grandpa and you come and visit me."

Practice the habit of smiling.
April 23

TONIGHT AS WE WERE EATING SUPPER Luverne said, "One thing I've noticed that I think we want to guard against."

"Poor posture?" I queried.

"That," he agreed, "but also the downward turn of the mouth. It gives such a dour look to the face."

Anticipating Sister Vicki's visit.
April 25

I AM MEETING WITH SISTER VICKI only once or twice a month now, but remain grateful for her companionship on my journey. This summer she will make a trip to Ireland; and we have planned that after she returns she will spend a few days here with us.

Joseph.
May 3

LUVERNE WAS SWEEPING THE WALK this morning when Joseph came out of his house and headed for his car, staggering and weaving. Alarmed, Luverne hurried to his side, asking if he could help.

"I'm going to the hospital," Joseph said.

"Let me take you."

Joseph hesitated momentarily, then said, "All right. But wait a minute. I have to go into the house."

Luverne came running back home, told me he was taking Joseph to the hospital and asked me to come along so he could drop the two of us at emergency while he parked the car.

I ran out with Luverne. The door to Joseph's house stood open. We called. No answer. Luverne hurried down the hall. The odor I associate with cancer hit me full force as I stepped inside the house. Sickened, I backed out. Luverne came running back, saying Joseph was hermorraghing; there was blood all over.

One of our neighbors had popped in.

"Call 911!" I shouted, "Get an ambulance—quick!"

Fifteen minutes passed before the paramedics arrived, then a hook and ladder truck, and finally an ambulance. Our short street, newly named after the duplexes were built, is not marked on any city maps yet, thus the delay.

Luverne and I followed the ambulance in our car. I stood at the emergency door as the aides wheeled in Joseph on a gurney. Once inside I offered him my hand. He clutched it tightly.

Examining him quickly, the doctors gave orders to admit him.

Luverne had rejoined us, and we walked alongside Joseph's gurney as the attendants rolled it down the hall.

"I've walked these halls a thousand times," Joseph blurted out. "Where are they sending me? Oncology? That's where Ethel was until she died. Only a year and a half ago. Oh, God!"

Settled finally in his bed, Joseph's carefully shored-up reserves crumbled. The dam burst; sobs poured out.

"I knew it would come, but oh, how I had hoped it wouldn't! I really wasn't ready for it."

"None of us are, Joseph."

"We had to wait eight years to be accepted at Pilgrim Place. Then while we were waiting for a house, Ethel's cancer reoccurred, and she died. That meant I had to enter as a single." He paused, then went on.

"The house offered me was so small. No study. I had writing I wanted to do. So I applied to go the route of builder/applicant—pay for the building, hoping I could live in it for a few years. I knew it was a gamble, but I had hoped so much . . . But to have it end so soon!"

"The fight isn't over yet, Joseph."

"I wish I could believe that. I want so much to live."

We sat with Joseph a while longer, then came home, cleaned his house, aired it, and did the laundry. Luverne took his trousers to the dry cleaner.

We returned to the hospital at 5:30. As we sat with him, Joseph began to relive his years spent in what was then known as the Congo, speaking with animation, betraying how much those years had meant to him. After a while, seeing that he had wearied, we said good night and promised to come back tomorrow.

Heavy of heart, I sought healing when we came home by puttering around in our little garden. Luverne suggested we go out for Chinese food, but we couldn't finish what we had ordered. Of our eleven we're the only two left at home this evening on Cambridge Way. All the other houses are dark, and our little neighborhood feels empty.

Signs of hope.
May 4

*J*OSEPH APPEARED MORE CHEERFUL when we visited him today.

Joseph.
May 5

*W*HEN WE VISITED JOSEPH this afternoon we learned from the nurse that he had hemorrhaged three more times. Joseph had been talking about Esther, his wife's sister, who lives in Colorado. On the way home I asked Luverne if he thought we should call Esther. Luverne agreed. This evening when we visited Joseph he told us he had called Esther and asked her to come. She was inquiring about flights.

Esther.
May 7

We picked up Esther at the airport this afternoon, took her first to Joseph's house, where she will stay, and then to the hospital, telling her we would return at 5:30 to pick her up and bring her here for supper. What a lovely person in every way she appears to be: possessing the quiet, unpretentious, unassuming charm of a gentlewoman from old-world Europe.

As we were eating supper Esther said, "Joseph asked me to tell you that he will welcome you whenever you can come, and he would like you to feel free to stay as long as you can or wish."

Jessie and Rex.
May 15

JOSEPH IS BACK FROM THE HOSPITAL and is staying now in the Health Services Center. Esther keeps daily vigil by Joseph's side. I grope to describe adequately her caregiving: tireless, compassionate, skillful, gentle, patient, unselfish, understanding. But all caregivers need time off, and so some of us take turns sitting with Joseph. I go frequently.

Spending time in the Health Services Center with Joseph is introducing me to some of the other residents as I see them walking in the halls or passing the door of Joseph's room. One couple walks past daily, hand in hand. She shuffles unsteadily; he buoys her lovingly. Sometimes he coaxes her outside; sometimes they sit together in the lounge. He watches TV; her eyes move restlessly. When she curls up on the davenport and falls asleep, he does not leave her, but settles behind a card table and works on a jigsaw puzzle. Sometimes she prattles senselessly—at least I can't make sense of it; but her husband seems to understand, and not only her every word, but every movement of her body, every expression of her face.

I asked Joseph about them yesterday. He told me they were pilgrims, Rex and Jessie Knowles by name.

The battle with a sense of worthlessness.
May 16

JOSEPH WAS "DOWN" TODAY. He complained that he wasn't good for anything anymore, that he couldn't do anything, that he never would be able to do anything again.

I listened then moved over to the patio door and stood looking outside. After a while he asked me what I was thinking about. I told him he doesn't like being preached at. He was silent and then said, "Well, I could try it." I said no. I heard a chuckle, then, "Oh, come on. Just once."

I waited, then turning, walking up to his bed and looking him in his eye—kindly, I hoped—I said, "Joseph. What we *are* is far more important than anything we *do*."

Silence. A steady gaze returned. Then, "Thank you, Millie."

No more gloomies, at least for today. But I certainly can understand his feelings. Who of us hasn't felt the same?

Thanking God for memories.
May 18

WHEN I MET REX IN THE LOUNGE today he took a piece of paper out of his pocket and handed it to me. Unfolding it and glancing at it, I asked, "You write poetry?"

He shrugged. "Call it what you wish. It helps to try to write out some of my feelings."

I started to read, but before I had come to the end the words were blurring for me.

Alzheimer's

The song-spun dream has fled.
She sits, withdrawn, her gentle face
disguising empty thoughts.

She holds my hand, but does she know?
For forty years she made my life poetry.
She knew it. I told her
   and showed her daily.
     I still owe her thirty-four.
For six years now, where has she been?

Love is there, for I love,
   I dearly love—even the empty shell.

But the song-spun dream that
   was dreamed so many years ago has fled.

Thank God for a life of memories of a lovely melody.
Thank God for a hand to hold now.

I handed the paper back to Rex. What could I say? I also was thinking of my stupid mistake in assuming men aren't aware of and don't know how to express their feelings. Rex interrupted my musings by saying he was lucky. Jessie's inner core of gentleness, joy, and love continue to shine through from time to time, he said. He admitted she sometimes gets agitated, but usually she is playful.

"I've learned some things," he said, "never to approach her from the back, but to stand directly in front of her, or better yet, kneel, and look in her eyes. I refrain from touching if she draws back. I offer my hand; if she accepts it, I pat it gently. Fleeting moments of recognition and response come occasionally, rewarding me immensely. For example, I was wheeling her down the hallway one day. An aide bumped into her and apologized profusely. Jessie said loud and clear, 'It was only an accident.'

"One day the grandchildren came. I began to review their names: 'This is Mark, this . . .' Then pointing to myself, I said, 'This is It Stinks.' Jessie responded immediately with, 'Oh, no!' I'm learning," he concluded, "that the deepest joys are not so much spectacular as ordinary."

"I'm learning," I said, "that one cannot really help if one does not love."

Welcoming gentle spring.

May 19

𝒩O CLOUDS DARTED across the sky today as I viewed it through the budding and leafing-out vista of the trees in our neighbor's yard. Deep sapphire blue the sky was. One of the peaks of the San Gabriel Mountains still veils itself with an undulating blanket of snow. I felt like shouting at it that it was time for it to cast aside its shroud; all nature is breaking out in spring.

Closer at hand, on the other side of the cement block wall separating us from our neighbor, fruit trees are beginning to bud. My eyes rested on our own little ribbon of garden. The rosebushes are developing buds. Some of the gladiola have begun to push their spearlike heads above the soil. The fringed Martha Washington geraniums glow brilliantly with their deep violet blooms accentuated by the white hanging pots that hold them.

These few quiet moments when I stand at our bedroom patio door every morning and look out fall as a gentle benediction; and this morning stepping outside I breathed deeply, and then I heard the birds tuning up for their symphonies: long successions of rapid chirps followed by joyous trills. And I said to myself, "It's good to be alive!"

Command

> *Sing, O thou, my soul!*
> *Sing the joyous canticle*
> *which burns within your depths—*
> *Each word a flame*
> *enkindled by the showering sparks*
> *of Love itself . . .*
> *fanned by Living Breath*
> *unto that*
> *roaring, soaring*
> *rumbling, tumbling*
> *torrent of praise which o'erwhelms*
> *unto a hushed—unending*
> *SILENCE*

Each melody—
   not separate, disjointed strains
   but one unending flow
   of heart's love—ceaselessly changing—
   one unto another,
   Yet unbroken, in ever-increasing intensity,
      quickened, heightened, unto a
breathless repose of adoring
      SILENCE.

Oh sing, my soul,
   Sing unto Thy God!
      —Mary K. Himens, SSCM

Good-bye to Freddie.
May 22

JOSEPH IS ILL. We continue to visit him, but at the same time life—ordinary, everyday life—continues on for us with its prosaic events. Today Luverne pulled Freddie, our tent trailer, to the home of a friend who will store and use it until Judy and her husband can tow it to their home in northern California.

With sadness I watched it disappear around the corner. Every summer while the children were growing up, we would pack it up and take off on a vacation trip. Now those days are gone. We'll continue to travel but in a different way. I'll miss the streams and forests in the midst of which we formerly parked, the chattering brooks and sighing pines that lulled me to sleep, and the chirping and trilling of birds that awakened me.

"For everything there is a season," the writer of Proverbs wrote. Yes, yes, I know, but this is one season I shall miss.

The doctor admitted Joseph to the hospital this afternoon to begin radiation treatment.

A surprise anniversary gift.
May 23

Our wedding anniversary. A sunny morning. I spent a few moments outside surveying the progress our flowers are making. Then we walked to Ken and Barbara's, residents who had invited us and four others for a 7:30 A.M. breakfast with waffles, all the trimmings, and lots of steaming hot coffee and tea.

Our conversation traversed many subjects. At 9:00 our party broke up. The breakfast had added a lovely celebrative touch to our special day. With Ken and Barbara not knowing it was our anniversary, the invitation had come as a surprise gift. Nothing helps me more to feel I belong here than to be invited to a home.

After breakfast we drove to the hospital to see Joseph. A disturbed, uncomfortable night had not allowed him to sleep. It hurts to see him suffer.

Then we headed for apple country in the mountains. Maybe we can find some apple trees and lilac bushes in bloom, we said to each other. At our wedding in Minnesota thirty-eight years ago, we had banked our church with large white baskets filled with lilac and apple blossoms. Wouldn't it be fun, I said, to bring home a bunch of lilacs? But the only two bunches we found all day were drooping, so abandoning the idea, we headed for the village, where in one of our favorite coffee shops we splurged on the apple pie for which it is famous. When the waitress asked us if today was a special day for us and we told her, she piled on huge chunks of ice cream. Yum! One of the elder women interviewed for the book *When I Get Old I Shall Wear Purple* declared that getting old meant to her, among other things, eating food not good for her—at least occasionally! I think that is a delightful idea.

Music, conversation, and silence enhanced our freeway drive home, but what brought us the most contentment and gratitude was the fact that we still have each other. We loved each other the day we married; we love each other in a far deeper and more complete way now.

Had it been a perfect day? I hesitate to use that word. Happy, yes, in one sense, but how could it be perfect overshadowed as it was by Joseph's illness and suffering?

Not only the elderly live with uncertainty.
May 28

SEVERAL MONTHS AGO we signed up to attend a weekend family camp in the mountains which took place this past weekend. With Joseph so ill we were reluctant to go, but Esther urged us, saying with Joseph in the hospital there was little we could do for him. So we went and returned home last night.

Conversing with people there gave me new insight to life today for many people. The first evening a young couple for whom marriage is a second venture sat down at our supper table. The man is into his third career. He said he loves what he is doing now but knows that in five years his job quite likely will be obsolete, and he will have to train for something else. I tried to guess how old he is. Forty-five at the most perhaps?

A single mother with two young children who had joined us at our table said she has retrained twice and now another company has just bought her company, and she didn't know what the future holds for her. "I used to say," she said, "that I need to have two months' salary in savings to tide us over if I lost my job. I know now I need a year's. That's a lot for one like me."

An older woman, a widow for many years, who was sitting across from us, spoke up. She said that last week she was talking to her daughter about the homeless; and her daughter had said quietly that she was only one month away from being homeless herself. She already had been forced to cancel the family's health insurance; and she said if she lost her job, even with her husband working, they wouldn't be able to make insurance and car payments, pay the rent, buy groceries and gas. She asked which of these they could do without.

The next day, as I was sitting on a bench outside, an eight-year-old joined me.

"We're going to have to move to a smaller apartment next month," she confided. "Mom says we can't afford the one we're in now. She lost her job. Her company told her they had found people who'd work for less than she would."

"How do you feel about moving?"

"Don't like it! Not one little bit! I have three little brothers, and now we'll all have to be in one room together." She sighed. "Bunk beds. And what'll happen to all my toys? Mom says we're going to have to sell some of our furniture. Mom says you can't get much for used furniture." She drew a deep breath again. "No, I don't like it, but Mom says that's the way the cookie crumbles sometimes, that's the way life is sometimes."

During supper a man in his early fifties confided that he hoped he would be able soon to find a job. He had been unemployed seven months. He said all he wanted was to reach age 60.

Sunday morning a woman in her seventies came and sat on a bench under a tree where I was sitting. She told how after her husband died she moved to live close to two of her children, but their jobs have called them away from her. She hadn't wanted to move to a distant, strange city, so she stayed where she was; but, she said, sometimes she feels so alone now and as though her children and she are drifting farther and farther apart. "And I don't know my grand-children at all," she said sadly.

I sit tonight reflecting on all these conversations and note how all of us, regardless of which age group we find ourselves in, learn that while much in life is predictable, much is unpredictable. Causes have effects. The foundations of our life as a nation are shifting and moving with mobility of population, the influx of immigrants from many lands, demographic upheaval, the social shift of two-income families, and the urban shift from industrial to technology. These changes affect all of us.

Surrogate families and friends fill gaps on our special days.
June 6

WHAT A HAPPY BIRTHDAY I'VE HAD! One of our Cambridge Way neighbors suggested we get together for a potluck soup and salad supper tonight. At dessert time Hal walked in carrying an angel food cake encircled with rosy strawberries fresh from the field, a cake Luverne had baked. Then peals of laughter broke out when my thoroughly perplexed face greeted a second candle-bedecked cake, a double chocolate one. "Happy Birthday!" they sang.

And so today I am 70! But 70 still sounds ancient to me. I don't feel 70; I merely feel like Millie.

I wonder how brutally pain is twisting Joseph's body tonight.

Offering companionship for the last stretch.
June 7

$\mathcal{N}$OT HAVING SEEN JOSEPH for a few days, his appearance startled me when I walked into his room today. He is back in the Health Services Center after days in the hospital receiving radiation treatment for the cancerous tumors on his neck, treatment given with the hope that it will relieve some of the pain.

Joseph has lost twenty pounds in the last two weeks and fifty-four since the cancer took over aggressively. His eyes lie sunken in hollows; his teeth are pulling away from his gums; his wristwatch slides halfway up his forearm now. But his brown eyes still can twinkle mischievously, and he retains his contagious smile. His doctor says he knows Joseph is experiencing much more pain than he will admit. Joseph seldom talks about it; but before he went into the hospital, he did.

"What I feel here in my neck," reaching up to touch it carefully, he had said, "especially if I have to move, is, I suppose, what you'd call pain. It's sharp, stabbing fierce, like someone plunging a knife in me. What you call pain hovers over me constantly, only the medication keeps it from possessing me entirely. As for my body," his bony hands had passed over his frame covered only with a sheet, "it's different. I am conscious of my entire skeletal and muscular structure."

"Did the radiation help?" I asked this morning.

"I think so. I'm not hurting quite as much as before. But my throat is so sore. Give me only ice chips today," he begged.

An hour later he spoke. "Time carries a sense of ambiguity for me now. It's shortened drastically, but the days," he stopped to catch his breath, "the hours, the minutes, drag. Endlessly." Esther came to sit with Joseph, so this evening Luverne and I joined our pilgrim community gathered in Decker Hall to observe Memorial Day. Some retirement communities avoid the reality of death, I've been told. No announcements of death given. If the resident had not belonged to a church or a synagogue, even then no memorial service is held at the center.

Not here. As many pilgrims as are physically able attend memorial services, even when they have not known the deceased pilgrim well. "We are family, and family attend memorial services." Again and again I have heard this emphasized. I think of my friend Till and how she had to call and ask a few of us, her friends, to gather for her mother's service. That will never happen here.

And so tonight we came together again to remember those who have died the past year. A narrator read the names of the pilgrims and a brief eulogy, noting especially the contribution each had made to the community. Listening, I felt myself being born into this new extended family, a family I need to know better, a family that needs to know me better.

At the end of the service the pianist began to play, "There's a Land That Is Fairer Than Day"; and then as I heard soft humming beginning at the front of the hall and moving slowly back, surging and swelling like an ocean tide rolling into shore, I felt little bumps popping out on my arms. I walked out of the hall feeling I had been standing at the doorway of that land that our God has promised us will be "fairer than day."

We stopped to see Joseph on the way home; and he surprised us by saying, "I've arranged for a dinner for Luverne and you and Esther tomorrow night. You are to be at the Inn at 6:00 P.M. I've made all the reservations."

Evidently he saw my eyebrows drawing together in questioning, for his eyes twinkled; and he smiled as he reached over to touch his phone. "I still have a phone," he reminded me.

The young called him a sweetheart.

June 8

$\mathcal{W}$HEN WE ARRIVED at the restaurant this evening, the headwaiter was waiting for us. Other younger waiters clustered around to ask how Joseph was.

"He knew how fond I was of antiques," a tall, dark-haired youth said. "When he was dismantling his home, he gave me several old pieces I really treasure."

"Joseph was a sweetheart," the receptionist said.

Even though it was nine o'clock when we returned home, we slipped into the Health Services Center by the door we knew we would find open. Joseph was waiting for us.

Esther gave him the greetings from the waiters. "The receptionist said you're a sweetheart," I said. "Really, Joseph! I don't know about you!"

His impish smile flickered to the surface. He laughed softly. "You're too much," he said.

Suffering.

June 9

$\mathcal{T}$ODAY HAS BEEN A HORRIBLE DAY for Joseph. Was it a reaction to the morphine or his temperature—which climbed to almost 101 degrees—or both which sent him hallucinating?

"Get me scissors, quick!" he begged. "I'm bound with ropes!"

"You feel like you're tied, but you aren't, Joseph," I tried to reassure him. "You're free. You feel the way you do because of a reaction to the medication."

He tried to tear off his gown and fling himself to the floor. We had to hold him in. Poor Joseph! I thought relief would never come. When he finally slid into—sleep? unconsciousness?—I slipped out into the hallway to wander aimlessly back and forth. Rex came upon me in my wanderings.

"You remarked the other day that both living and dying sometimes can be lonely," he said.

I nodded mutely.

He reached in his shirt pocket, took out a folded piece of paper, and handed it to me.

"Loneliness," I read, and then:

> *Loneliness grows.*
> *It started within me*
> *and expanded until it filled me.*
> *And it spilled over*
> *until it was not only in me*
> *but all around me.*
> *It grew with me.*
> *Even when I was with people,*
> *it surrounded me.*
> *Even with friends*
> *it encircled me.*
> *I cannot escape it.*
> *It grows, it swells, it expands*
> *until it is not in me,*
> *I am in it.*
> *And no matter how hard I try*
> *I cannot get out.*

"Watching a person slowly die isn't easy, is it?" I said.

"Agonizing—at least for me. I come home from a morning here, collapse in my chair, and fall asleep. But then I wake up refreshed and can go to Abernethy for dinner.

"Going through an experience like this . . . there are ups and downs. Things go quite well, then I hit a terrible time. Finally I have to set myself down and say, 'Now this is the way it is, so you're going to get through it.' And things get better and level out; and I live on that plateau for a while until . . .usually it's until I notice the next drop in Jessie's deterioration, and then it begins all over again."

"How ever do you cope?"

"I come home at night and review the day with God and with Jessie. I talk about the good points and confess the times I've failed and ask forgiveness. And then I go to bed and sleep. . . . How's Joseph?" he asked.

"Not good."

"I'm sorry." His tone told me he truly was. And he left.

I stood and stared out the window and stared and stared. Sometimes I feel as all the pain, sorrow, and loneliness of the Health Services Center, a minute microcosm of the suffering of the world, is going to devour me.

I re-enter Joseph's room. He lies, mouth slightly agape, his breathing rapid, but he is quiet. O God, grant him sleep tonight.

Joseph at the threshold and at peace.
June 10

JOSEPH LIES QUIETLY in bed today; he sleeps most of the time, or does he sleep? He lies with eyes half shut. Unseeing?

He recognizes people but rarely speaks. He makes few requests. He doesn't want to eat.

"You don't have to eat, Joseph."

"No visitors, please." A long silence, then, "Yesterday was a nightmare—a sea of faces."

We step out of the room, post a "No Visitors" sign on the door. He drifts off to sleep and after a while awakens. "Take the spread off."

We fold it back.

"Take it all off—the sheet too."

We fold the sheet back.

"Tell us if you feel cold, Joseph."

It's four o'clock now. Sounds from outside invade the room. Out in the hall an elderly visitor in a quavering voice visits with a patient. The woman in the wheelchair who has lost touch with reality wheels past, and just outside our room lets out such a loud, "Help!" I jump. She wheels down the hall a little and then yells again. Six times she lets out that "Help!"

Another woman, pushing a wheelchair, stops an aide in the hallway and asks, "Where is my room? Can anyone tell me where my room is?"

Another begs, "Will you put me to bed?"

I hear another, presumably at the nurses' station, chatting companionably. "I found someone to cut my toenails today," she says happily.

Our patio door, open to the outside, lets a cool, gentle breeze blow in. A plane far overhead drones on its way. The merry song of a mockingbird interrupts the droning. But over and above and permeating all these sounds is the sound of Joseph's labored breathing.

I have pulled my chair next to the bed, so Joseph can reach out for my hand if he wishes to do so, although these days he hasn't reached for it as often as before.

I am so weary! My head is full of tears that won't come. I am so, so tired. I lay my head down by Joseph on the bed.

Prayer

Help of the tired ones,
I am in need tonight—
so weary I can hardly think
or pray aright;
but you have known the toil,
the grief, the strain
of human suffering,
and felt the pain
of utter weariness—
the sting of tears, fatigue—
and so you know my need.

I have no words to say,
but in my heart
I pray.
                              —Mary Esther Burgoyne

6:00 P.M.

£STHER HAS GONE HOME TO EAT. The nurse comes into the room to tell me the doctor has prescribed medication for the fungus that has furred Joseph's throat and tongue. He also wants to give Joseph some slow-releasing morphine in tiny tablet form. The medication, the nurse says, will have to be sent from Pasadena; so it will take three hours to come.

9:30 P.M.

THE MEDICATION FOR THE THRUSH proves to be of a thin gelatin-type consistency which Joseph is to put in his mouth and swish around. It doesn't swish easily. After several unsuccessful tries, Joseph exclaims in his voice weakened but still capable of expression, "They had to send all the way to Pasadena for *this*?"

So unexpected is his remark we break out in laughter. A low rumble of a chuckle comes from Joseph too. What indomitable humor the man possesses!

Joseph has lost so much weight his wedding band threatens to slip off his finger.

"We could tape it on," I say to Esther.

"I don't want tape on the ring," Joseph pipes up. "Use the tape to tape shut the mouth of that woman who yells, "Help!"

Again, we cannot refrain from laughing.

Waiting.
June 11

THANK GOD, today passed more easily for Joseph. On my way home I met one of our Cambridge Way family.

"Joseph asked me the other day how one dies," he said. He paused. "I didn't know what to say. Told him I didn't know, haven't done it. Finally said I guess one just places oneself in God's hands and lets go."

Working out grief.

June 12

$\mathcal{J}$OSEPH DIED AROUND THREE O'CLOCK this morning. Esther called us; she had just received the call. We dressed quickly and went down to the Health Services Center. We held each other. Together we wept. Together we said good-bye to Joseph. Today, as is so often true when I experience loss of some kind, I found relief in physical work. I scrubbed the kitchen and bathroom floors on hands and knees and later scoured the shower and shower door. I bleached my towels; I pulled weeds in the garden. As I worked I thought how strange life and death are. Yesterday Joseph was alive, able to handle his own urinal, ask for chipped ice, for a cold cloth for his face. He smiled. He even joked. Around 4:30 he asked for a pad and pencil. He wanted to write something, but all he could do was make scratches.

Not alone.

June 15
The day of Joseph's funeral

$\mathcal{1}$ AM CRYING TODAY. I have held in check most of my crying these past weeks, but today I cry.

I cry because, although I believe in the resurrection, I have lost a friend, a friend who allowed me to know and love him, who gave me the gift of himself, his courage, and his humor, who accepted the little I had to give him, and thus, in the three—the learning to know him, in the receiving, and in the giving—I have found meaning in my being here during this uneasy time of transition.

The moon is only a thin sliver through the trees tonight. When I was out watering our little garden, the mosquitoes, who can always find me, clustered thirstily around my legs.

Ninety-year-old Nikki had said to me yesterday, "If you want flowers, come to my house and pick daisies. They need to be picked, and I can't pick them."

So I walked across the campus and came home with a bouquet.

Luverne has been gone since Wednesday, back in the Midwest cele-

Luverne has been gone since Wednesday, back in the Midwest celebrating the forty-fifth year of his ordination with his friends. One needs to keep friendships in repair; and when he bought his ticket, we didn't know Joseph would die while he was gone.

I missed my loved one today; I miss him tonight. On days like this I need arms to hold me, to comfort me. Distance, work, and cost kept him absent from my side when Mother and my sister died too. I missed him at that time also.

Joseph, what is it like after one dies? How much does one know? I feel your presence so close to me. What a mystery life and death and the spirit world are!

I'm crying again.

A child's concept of happiness.
June 20

When we arrived at Judy's, five-year-old Alison and three-year-old Reed jumped up and down and spoke all in a rush, words tumbling all over each other as they told us about the dinosaur birthday cake they had helped their mom bake and decorate to celebrate Grandpa's birthday.

That evening at story time after we had read some stories to them, Alison said, "I want to tell a story"; and she began.

"Once upon a time there was a woman named Judy and a man named Barry. They were lonesome, so they prayed to God way up there," sweeping her arms heavenward, "and God sent them a little girl, and she was Alison." Pause, then: "But they were still lonesome, so they prayed again to God way up there [more arm sweeping] . . . ," and on and on she continued until she had named her brother, her two best friends, and her cousins. Then she paused, propped her chin in the palm of one hand in a dramatic posture of deep thought. Finally she roused herself with a deep breath and continued, "They were *still* [heavy emphasis placed on 'still'] lonesome. So they prayed to God way up there, and the wind began to blow; and it blew and it blew and it blew until it blew the clouds apart, and Grandpa and Grandma came down; and after that none of them were lonesome anymore." She paused, drew another long breath, and concluded, "And after that they all lived together happily in a great big shoe!"

Loneliness. I thought of little Alison's story and the fairy-tale ending she gave it when she proclaimed happily, "and then they weren't lonesome anymore!"

A little five-year-old could recognize and identify the gaping, empty hole in the soul. In her innocence she perceived warm, intimate, human relationships able to meet that need.

Oh, little Alison, you, along with many others, have yet to learn that even the most caring, supportive people are inadequate when it comes to filling that empty space in the heart placed there by God. Only God can fill that hole.

The Psalmist knew that. The Psalmist, in exile, feeling abandoned and forsaken cried out,

> *As a doe longs*
> *for running streams,*
> *so longs my soul*
> *for you, my God.*
>
> *My soul thirsts for God,*
> *the God of life;*
> *when shall I go to see*
> *the face of God?*
>
> *I have no food but tears,*
> *day and night;*
> *and all day long men say to me,*
> *"Where is your God?*
> (Psalm 42:1-3)*

"I am," the Psalmist cries out, "like a doe, standing by a rock-strewn stream that has dried up, so thirsty that my tongue hangs out as I pant for the water I need to keep me alive."

For me also it is during the times of dryness of soul that torture me that I, an everlastingly thirsty soul, discovering all else fails, in desperation turn to God. And God *always* hears my cry even though the time of drought might continue yet a little longer.

These lessons lie far down the road for you to learn, Alison, my sweet little granddaughter. For now, delight in and feel loved and secure in the love your parents and we offer you.

Widened vision.

July 1

1 DECIDED THIS MORNING to become better acquainted with some of the many facets of life here at Pilgrim Place.

I headed first for Pendleton, the arts and crafts building. Here on different days weavers sit at their looms interlacing warp and threads; potters spin their wheels and fire their kiln; stained-glass artisans carefully cut and fit glass in frames; woodworkers saw, sand, and shape chests, dollhouses, footstools; artists stroke the canvas on their easels with their brushes; a sculptor molds lovingly the bust she is creating; a lapidary cuts and polishes precious stones; and women busily fashion decorative items for holiday use. The building today hummed contentedly with the buzz and whine of saws, the soothing melodies of classical music softly played and the low murmur of voices.

I asked some of the workers if they had learned and practiced their art before they came here. Some said yes; others said they learned it after coming. I marveled.

In addition to the joy these artists experience in creating, added meaning comes because they will offer their creations for sale at the festival, knowing that the income will be used to provide for those whose resources do not stretch far enough to cover today's costs for care.

Leaving the building, I walked down the road a short distance to the Festival Building where several committees work. In one room some women were sorting and pricing items crafted overseas to offer for sale in the International Bazaar Booth. Here too I saw stored some of the costumes used for the play portraying the arrival of the pilgrims to the U.S. Next door in a book-lined room a couple of men were sorting and pricing used books. One told me income from these books alone will total over $14,000.

Adjacent to the used-books room another huge room acts as a storage and sorting space for hundreds of donated miscellaneous items. A man was repairing a toaster.

"We spend hundreds of hours getting everything sorted, cleaned, and in good order," a woman told me. "But when we can net over $15,000, $17,000, we feel immensely rewarded."

In an adjacent room I saw donated used furniture which newly arrived pilgrims or staff workers may purchase.

Moving on from the Festival Building, I walked along a curving road until I came to a nook tucked away next to a garage where some women were busily at work designing and printing silk-screen note cards. Close by in a semi-basement area I found others sorting and repairing costume jewelry, while some labeled homemade jams. In yet another section four were unpacking boxes sent over from estate settlements and sorting the contents: fine linens to be given to the linens committee, silver, china, and crystal to be polished as needed and then appraised for sale.

What I saw on my morning walk impressed on me afresh that leisure activities need to be more than mere hobbies; they must bring meaning to life. As I was thinking about this—I was still in the semi-basement room—one of the workers directed a question to me. Did I have special interests? Stamp collecting? Coins? Gardening? Did I play a recorder? A stringed instrument? Sing?

Would I like to be a receptionist at the Health Services Center or be a docent at the museum? Perhaps I'd like to drive people to the market or doctor's office? One offered to give me a list of the over thirty committees working for the festival. Someone had heard I write; would I like to work on the newsletter? Did I enjoy flower arranging? Or gardening? Raising plants?

My head was beginning to whirl, and then I noticed their smiles and caught on that they were good-naturedly joking with me. Relieved,

I thanked them for all their suggestions and said I really had to leave. "Take your time in deciding what you might enjoy doing. I think we should allow new residents a year of freedom," one said.

I smiled her my appreciation, thanked them for the visit, and left, having decided I had done enough exploring.

20/20 vision.

July 2

"HAVE YOU EVER MET a group with so many wide and varied interests?" I asked Luverne this afternoon as we were walking home from Abernethy. We had just sat through half a dozen announcements about speakers who would be coming, activities being planned, and meetings we could attend.

"Nicaragua, Cuba, Argentina, Russia, Mexico, China, Burma, Japan, Hong Kong, economics, the environment, South Africa, status of women, process theology, World War II, current movies being shown, taxes, Habitat for Humanity, Heifers International, the United Nations, battered women, child labor, AIDS, mediating for the rights of farm-workers, world affairs—what topic isn't discussed? And all the different interest groups: Women's Perspective, the Andiron Club, the Chorale, the Recorder Group, the Play Readers, the Committee on Social Action, on Peace and Justice, on World Affairs, Amnesty International, and the book clubs—I could spend all my time attending meetings or working on committees right here.

"Then as I listen in at the tables, I hear some talking about" I counted on my fingers as I spoke, "prison ministry, caring for the homeless, tutoring children, teaching Bible classes, working with the League of Women Voters, the Red Cross. Some of the men, I've gathered, serve as chaplains at care centers and some as interim pastors. I think a few have even traveled overseas for interims. Talk about a busy bunch of people!

"But, Honey, think of Joseph. What will it be like for them when health and physical energy do not allow them to continue active?"

"They'll adapt," Luverne said. "Joseph did. They've lived their lives finding meaning, and they are facing the future with eyes wide open too. They wouldn't be here if they weren't."

Evening

$\mathcal{T}$HE DAY IS OVER. I am not handling this transition well. I find myself rebelling against the thought of continuing to spend my years busy, busy, busy. I had envisioned giving some hours to volunteer work and some to socializing, certainly. But I also want opportunities to continue learning, to think, reflect, to record my life pilgrimage. Time to spend with our children and grandchildren. To travel as finances allow. Time to read, listen to music, visit museums, see good movies.

At the same time I know communities like this vivify only because everybody contributes something. But how can I make a contribution and at the same time not be swallowed up?

The day has quivered with heat; but now as I stand in the doorway the evening coolness, the spaciousness of the star-studded heavens above, and the healing quietness all around call me to come out. And so I shall head off. Ned, one of our new friends has invited me to come and pick roses whenever I wish.

Later, back home

$\mathcal{W}$HAT A LOVELY TIME I'VE HAD! As I walked, the cool night breezes ruffled my hair. Somewhere in the near distance an owl hooted. I decided to take a circuitous route to Ned's house.

On the way I passed a family of mother cat and kittens who amused me for a while.

Many pilgrims leave their draperies open at night, inviting me to look in. I saw friends playing cards, a grandmother and a young girl putting together a puzzle, a weary one asleep in a rocking chair, book open on his lap, reading glasses on his nose.

How unusual, I thought, in metropolitan L.A. to find this small-town, friendly neighborly environment.

Finally I came to Ned's garden. Here the roses perfumed the night air. I breathed deeply. The moon offered me enough light to walk among the roses, enjoying each one. I selected a yellow bud and clipped it. With it in hand, not ready yet to go inside, I searched for and found a bench in a secluded spot and sat down to watch the swiftly changing cloud formations overhead. Then I began to talk over the day with my God. I lingered so he could speak to me. Finally at peace I came home.

Gull-Like

So often this is how I am—
  caught between the land and sea,
  hesitant to move, doubtful, and quizzical
  about which way, and how, and why.

So I stand fixed, as rooted in the now moment
  as if there were no past to give me reason,
  and no future to give me hope.

God lives in Eternal-Now-Ness.
  So I've been told, and do believe, I think!
Perhaps this perplexing moment, this "now"
  is some unfathomable gift,
  a "now' in which to share
  the "NOW" of His own "NOW-NESS"?
    —Mary K. Himens, SSCM

The soul at rest hears God's voice.
July 5

$\mathcal{A}$ND ONCE AGAIN MY FAITHFUL GOD has met my need in my evening's readings. From Richard Foster's *Celebration of Discipline*: "True service comes from a relationship with the divine Other deep inside. We serve out of whispered promptings, divine urgings." He goes on to state that true service quietly and unpretentiously cares for the needs of others, putting no one under obligation to return the service, drawing, binding, healing, building, and resulting in unity of community.

And then in his book *Learn to Grow Old* Paul Tournier stated that surrendering his life to God never meant turning his back on the world. "Rather," he wrote, "it meant investing myself in it "in a wider and deeper way. Nor did it mean that I gave up action. What I was giving up was my claim to act in accordance with my own will, in order to allow myself to be led as much as possible by God."

Even though at times I have missed God's nudgings, still I have sought all my life to "serve out of whispered promptings, divine urgings." I have sought to allow God to lead me. I shall continue to walk this path; for, as Tournier promises, if I do so, I shall find "considerable relaxation of tension," and be able to surrender to God even all the worry about the things I have left uncompleted. That would bring genuine rest of heart. Oh, God, I pray:

> *Drop thy still dews of quietness,*
> *Till all our strivings cease;*
> *Take from our souls the strain and stress,*
> *And let our ordered lives confess*
> *The beauty of thy peace.*
> —*John G. Whittier, 1807-1892*

Part Two:
Anchoring In God

You can never go home again.

July 7

Cleaning the parsonage where Ron and Janet will be living while Ron does his internship in this church has brought me back to Minneapolis in the land of sky-blue waters. Many years ago when I went to college and later worked here I had known the church and congregation to be two of the finest of its denomination in the city. What I had not realized before arriving here yesterday was how drastically the neighborhood has changed. The church now has become an inner-city church in a mixed ethnic and racial neighborhood. The brick church building and the parsonage still remain as imposing as I had remembered them, but all the surrounding houses, elegant in their time, now stand decrepit, drab, and dilapidated.

Cries in the night.

July 8

What a horrible night last night was! I was lying in bed still awake when a woman's cries shot me straight up in bed.

"Ohh . . . Ohh . . . Stop! Stop!" she was crying. Her pleading cries mounted and then erupted in a scream. I heard a door slam, and then a man's voice yelled, "You can't get away from me."

I jumped out of bed, heart thumping like it's never thumped before, ran to my bedroom window and kneeling, peered down. In the pale moonlight I saw a woman on the ground and a man straddling her. Stooping down and picking her up, he flung her against the side of the house. She shrieked, then lay there whimpering and moaning.

Janet and Ron came running from their bedroom and leaning over me looked down at the scene below. The man pounded the woman with his fists, kicked her with his boot. She groaned and wailed, begging for mercy. Then her laments died, and she lay limp and still.

"Oh, my God!"—it was a prayer, not an expletive—from Janet. "This is awful, awful!"

The man straightened and looked up at our window. We ducked out of sight. Ron inched back and then sailed down the stairs. We could hear him dialing. Did the man see Ron at the phone? Perhaps, for he picked up the woman and half carrying, half dragging her, he hauled her in the house. By the time the flashing red lights of the police car began to sweep the area, all was quiet; and the searching lights revealed only a house with a closed door.

"Let's crawl into our room," Janet whispered. "It's on the other side of the house. They can't see us there."

Both Janet and I were trembling violently. We sat on the floor in Janet and Ron's room and tried to empty our minds of the brutal violence we had witnessed.

Around two in the morning I crawled back to my room; but when I stood up to ease myself back into bed, I found my legs weak and insecure under me. The humid heat of the day still laid claim on the night, but I was shivering. Only sometime after four did I sleep.

Nicotine.

July 10

$\mathcal{I}$'VE BEEN CLEANING ALL DAY. The house undoubtedly considered grand and elegant in its day still remains so inside with the oak paneling, the hardwood floors, and the carved cornices. But the single men who lived here last year smoked, and so I am scrubbing all the woodwork and floors. Later I'll wash windows and clean the blinds. We'll have the carpets cleaned commercially. We must rid the house of the smell of nicotine which has permeated everything.

Taking time to sit on doorsteps and listen.
July 11

JANET, STILL RECOVERING from her siege with Guillain-Barré syndrome, tries to follow her doctor's order to rest in order to bring about full recovery. Minnesota's humid heat which has settled over the land keeps her indoors during the day; but toward evening when it begins to cool down a little, she ventures out and sits on the steps of the back porch. The little children of the neighborhood, having discovered her, come over, squat on the steps beside her or on the ground at her feet, and talk.

"My Mom's out of it again, lying half off, half on the sofa."

"Who will cook for you tonight?" Janet asks.

The little girl shrugs. "Dunno. Maybe me."

"My ma and pa fight all the time. Real loud. Scares me. I run to the basement and hide."

"My dad took off, don't know where he went. Just left."

"Happened to us too. Another man is living with us now, but he's not my dad."

"The police came last night and hauled my mom away."

Janet recounts these tales to me; and eleven, twelve o'clock at night, as I lie sleepless in bed, I hear the children running in the streets. Does no one care for, care about these children?

The contrast between this life and the secluded, protected life I know in Claremont where even trees are protected from being felled leaves me with so many mixed feelings that I shall need time to process them. How bewildering this is to me! This is the Midwest! This is life now in the city where I used to live!

Doing what we can.
July 12

RON TOLD ME AT LUNCH that the congregation is trying to meet the needs of this volatile, suffering community by offering classes to learn English as a second language, by providing a shelter for about one hundred homeless, a place of refuge for battered and raped women, and help in job searching for the unemployed. But the needs are so immense, the problems so great.

Replenish when need depletes you.
July 14

THE HOUSE IS REASONABLY CLEAN and finally free of tobacco odor. I am weary. Every bone and muscle in my body aches. My work here is finished.

Witnessing with my own eyes a cruel man beating a helpless woman and hearing with my own ears her unheeded pleas for help, and all this in a city that offered me relative safety and serenity in my youth has badly shaken me up. Viewing it on TV I can be comparatively dispassionate; this is different. And so when Luverne arrived last night I asked if he would take me to the North Shore. I asked if we could spend two or three days there. He quickly agreed.

In search of quietness.
July 15, the North Shore

EVENING IS CREEPING IN ON US GENTLY. We are spending the night in a bed-and-breakfast home. Perched in a window seat looking down through birch and evergreen, I gaze on the vast waters of Lake Superior. Huge, layered granite boulders at either end form a miniature bay below. The waters lap up on the beach quietly, reminiscent for me of the sheltered coves of the Indian Ocean at Mombasa. The six-hundred-foot-long beach below surprised us with a kaleidoscope of colors and shapes in the rocks that form the floor of the beach. Like children combing a seashore for shells we hunted rocks.

Today has been neither too warm nor too cool. The sun shown brightly, but the trees arching the trails where we walked sheltered us, allowing only dappled rays to filter through.

The scenes of the day play themselves again on the screen of my mind. I gloried in the rushing rivers tinged gold with the iron and copper veins that thread these rocky hills as I watched them cascade and plunge down waterfall after waterfall. We peered down awesome, black canyons, chasms in the earth, and most stupefying of all, in one place a huge open fault in the crust of the earth.

Discovering fragile, delicate wild roses caused memories of the rose-bushes that climbed the fences of the pastures on the farm of my childhood to flash back on the screen of my inner eye. I saw honeysuckle, baby breaths, bluebells and everywhere daisies, the daisies of my father's homeland of Sweden, loons calling, sea gulls swooping, Canada geese ducking for fish, an inexperienced one bellyflopping in its fish-catching attempts—I had reveled in all I saw.

I ask myself why I have come here. To escape? I hope not. But I need time to process what I have seen: the suffering, the staggering changes. I need time to gather courage again.

Dear God, how can you continue to bear the sins of the world? Why has your judgment not descended on us? How long-suffering and patient you are toward all of us! All this passes my understanding.

> *How often would I have gathered*
> *thy children together . . .*
> *(Matthew 25:37)*

> *Jesus,*
> *who looked over Jerusalem*
> *and wept with compassion*
> *and with grief,*
> *heart-broken*
> *by their unbelief,*
> *what do you do now?*

> *Nineteen hundred years ago*
> *there was no London*

hiding its tears
along the Embankment,
no New York Bowery
laughing in mockery
darkness till dawn,
no Calcutta,
stark, hunger-drawn.

O Jesus,
through two thousand years,
over our cities of deaf ears
your heart has yearned—
and still we have not learned.

"And ye would not . . ."

Could you have wept then
as you weep now,
as you must weep now?
                    —Mary Esther Burgoyne

A gift given for a time.

August 8, home again

1 CALLED TO TALK TO SISTER VICKI today to ask about her trip to Ireland to attend the wedding of her nephew and tell her how much I'm looking forward to her three-day visit here next week.

"You want to talk to Sister Vicki?" Silence. Then, "Oh, Millie, did we forget to call and tell you?"

"Tell me what?"

"Sister Vicki is dead."

"What?" I shouted into the phone.

"We don't have all the details. Her sister was driving. The car went in the ditch. Her sister had ribs broken, but Sister Vicki is dead. We are wondering if a heart attack killed her, but we don't know. She was buried in Ireland. We'll inform you when a date has been set for a memorial service here."

My heart is broken. At the beginning of our relationship Sister Vicki filled a unique role. She allowed me to confess my sins and did not minimize them or tell me I shouldn't feel or think or do what I had just confessed; she didn't say that it "was just natural," or say, "I'm sure we all do the same." No, she let the confession sit right out there in the open. Edna Hong, in her book *The Downward Ascent*, believes our enlightened, sophisticated, scientific age keeps busy "reconciling people to their sins and not to their God." Sister Vicki never did this; instead, after I had confessed, she very tenderly would ask if I wanted to pray. How often in her little prayer room the tears flowed! First tears of repentance, sorrow, and regret, then tears of relief and joy, because I knew God had forgiven me.

She bore patiently with me as I struggled through the Ignatian studies. She encouraged and affirmed me, although she rarely praised me, because she always believed I could do better. When I despaired, wondering if I'd ever write again, she reminded me that wounds slow us down, that dry times are often only fallow ground, being fertilized by time and the circumstances taking place. "Seeds are being sown," she would say. "Wait. At the right time the ideas will come. Then just let them come."

Affectionate, she always greeted me with "How are you, Love?" When we parted, she would hug and kiss.

She was an Olympic champion in spirituality, yet willing to mentor an ordinary person such as I. Profoundly spiritual though she was, common sense had strong roots in her too, and she could sniff out foolishness and nonsense a freeway exit away.

Nor did she lack humor. One day she dressed as a clown and danced into the old sisters' dining room, circling from table to table, tweaking the elderly sisters' noses, chucking them under their chins, kissing them. Completely befuddled, the reserved elderly sisters struggled not to let a smile, or worse yet, a hearty "haw-haw" disturb their sober, dignified miens. "It was so funny," Sister Vicki said when she told me.

When we moved here to Claremont, upon mutual agreement, our relationship changed from mentor-disciple to friend-friend. She requested it; I was honored to be asked.

I hope the next days to recall and write down my memories of Sister Vicki, so returning to them, she can live on for me. For now I must go to Abernethy for lunch. I pat my face with cold cloths first, then put my grieving on hold until I return home.

Wise mentor.
September 20

1 WOKE UP THIS MORNING thinking about Sister Vicki and how much I am going to miss her, but she would not want me grieving needlessly. Rather, she would want me to move intentionally toward healing and faithfully pursue enrichment of the spirit. Of this I am sure, and this I can do. This comforts.

In some ways, resolving this grief will be easier because Sister Vicki, wise mentor that she was, slowly had been weaning me away from dependence on her. Our relationship already had changed. We leaned on each other when we felt the need to do so, but more and more I have felt strong enough to stand on my own. For this I am grateful, and I shall forever be grateful that she came into my life when I needed her most. God is faithful.

Longing for stability.
September 28, Portland, Maine

*W*E FINALLY GOT TO BED at 11 P.M. last night after a turbulent flight on a thirty-passenger business express plane flying from Boston to Portland. Rain greeted us as we got off the plane. Finding one's way around in a strange city after dark presents a challenge. Then at 3 A.M. a friend calling from Canada, who thought we were in Portland, Oregon, awakened us!

We were glad the sun greeted us this morning. Our first stop today was Freeport. Gale-like winds were sending everyone's hair flying straight back like sails; but undeterred, people were crawling the streets which, in turn, caused traffic to crawl. Outlet stores, antique and craft shops of every kind lined the sidewalks for blocks, coaxing people to come inside, look, and buy, buy, buy. Did you need their products? Could you afford to buy them? What difference did it make? No state tax. Use your credit cards. Buy, buy, buy, just buy! This is just like California, I thought, and we escaped as quickly as we could.

We stopped at Bath to stretch our legs and walking around noticed immense, gray, windowless buildings stretching block after block. I asked a man clad in grubby work clothes standing on the sidewalk what the buildings were used for. He told us destroyers are built inside. I stared! I asked how many. He said he didn't know. He jerked his stubby finger in the direction of the harbor and said, "A couple are lying out there yonder."

We walked closer and looking at those monstrous, menacing, hippopotamic vehicles of destruction, lying motionless and silent now in the water, I shuddered and turned away quickly. My preconceived vision of a rural, unchanged, peaceful New England was beginning to fade. "Let's go," I said to Luverne.

When we emerged onto a highway that led us to a land of farms and small villages, I found myself beginning to relax as I feasted my eyes on ancient houses with house, garage, granary, and barn all joined together, on gingerbread houses painted white with green shutters and wrap-around porches and rockers on the porches and *people sitting in the rockers.*

Shuttered houses everywhere quietly made their statement that for a house to be well dressed, shutters are a must. I saw white houses with blue, gray, rust, sage green, black shutters. Cream-colored houses with rose, wine, and brown shutters. Light blue houses with white and bright green shutters. Yellow houses with green shutters.

Mid-morning we stopped at a tiny store on a side road. Inside, our glance took in some white plastic tables and chairs, a microwave for hot dogs, a sign telling us soft drinks, ice cream, and other snack foods were available. An elderly gentleman in a red-checkered flannel shirt and faded jeans held up with suspenders greeted us. We ordered a soft drink to share. The gentleman brought it to us at one of the plastic tables, then pulling up another chair sat down to talk.

I couldn't get the destroyers out of my mind. "The destroyers we saw in Bath," I said, "I thought the government was going to cut back on defense."

He shrugged. "That's what they tell you, what you read in the paper. But ask the folks in town. They'll tell you they've unfilled orders to fill and that they need the work." He regarded us carefully and then asked, "You visitors?"

We told him yes, it was our first trip to Maine.

"Leaf peepers?"

So that's what they call us who come to view fall foliage, I thought, chuckling to myself.

Then he started to tell us about himself. He was, he said, the eighth generation of his family to live on the land; his forebears came in 1630, traded with the Indians for 2,000 acres, but he has only 40 acres left now. Hard times forced him into logging for a time. His son had bought this store. He, the father, had hoped the son would farm the forty, but he's not interested, he said.

Maine, he said, is a poor state; people always have been poor. "In fact," he said with a wry smile, "so poor that when the Depression hit we didn't know the difference."

I didn't know how to respond. New Englanders, I guessed, don't want to be pitied even when they are struggling to make peace with all the changes occurring, so instead we thanked him for his hospitality and left.

As we continued on, we passed granite cliffs and grove after grove of trees. I took note of the delicate blue asters and lichen-covered moss.

Mid-afternoon we stopped again at a small wayside café and ordered a dish of ice cream to share. The man who brought it to us filled his mug with coffee and came and joined us.

I asked him if the birch, aspen, red and white spruce, balsam, fir, and quaking aspen we had seen were native to the area. He told us no, the trees we saw were not the ones that knew his grandfather's name but cash crops.

"When they cut the virgin forests, I cried," he said. "The trunks of those trees—three men could scarcely reach around their trunks." He pulled his lips together tightly, then went on, "But I soon learned if I was going to get food to eat, I better start logging."

Logging, he said, was sweaty work. They went out before sunup and stayed till sundown. Skinned knuckles, twigs in your eyes, bruised shins, cricks in your neck, aches in your back—"Do you think that's much fun?" he asked.

They slept in their clothes. Didn't bathe for weeks. Ate mostly beans and pea soup. The camps stunk. It was wickedly cold in the winter. From time to time to time wanigan boats brought supplies. The logs, he said, they floated downstream. Some would get stuck on sandbars, rocks. They'd bounce, scrape, roll, tumble all the way, get all their bark stripped off.

He got up, refilled his mug, and came back. "Polecats we'd call those who pushed the lumber along. Jills we'd call those fellows who didn't want to work; jillmocos those who worked but would go on a bender, sometimes desert."

My mind went scampering back to my father. I wondered if this was what life in a lumber camp had been like when he worked there for a brief time—feeling pity, compassion, and appreciation for him breaking out within. He had hated it.

Our companion was talking now about big logging trucks that haul seventy-ton loads. "Can you imagine the strain on the tires?" he asked. Knew one fellow about ten years ago who had two trucks and he paid $16,000 for tires alone that year. He wondered if tires were better now, but then maybe they cost more too.

Acadia National Park when we reached it late afternoon proved to be like a return visit to the St. Croix Valley of my homeland with its layered granite terrain. We are spending the night at Sommesville, a little town with less than four hundred residents.

Rusticators.

September 29

The TIDE WASHING IN awakened us this morning. As I lay listening to the swishing in and sucking back of the waves, memories flooded back to the first time I had heard those sounds when, in 1945 as a civilian on a troop ship, I traveled in convoy en route to India. At times in the 1940s, I thought, we seriously wondered if we were facing the end of a free civilization. Menacing, evil clouds hung luridly and threateningly over much of the world, but God had brought us through though only at the cost of much suffering and sorrow to humans—and also to God.

At noon we stopped at a country inn. A woman with sparsely growing gray hair, pulled back and knotted tightly in back, led us to a booth. She asked if we were visitors, then asked where we had come from. I told her and said last night I had enjoyed awakening to the swish of waves foaming into shore.

Sounds can carry ominous meanings for fishermen's wives left at home, she said. For them the sound of howling winds and crashing waves raises anxiety, and so does the absence of the sound of motors. "I know," she added, "I was one of those wives until my man died."

She disappeared to bring back a pot of coffee which she set down on our table. "Now, the sound of approaching storms and hurricanes and the alarms that go out for threatening floods, those sounds are a call to be human," she explained. To help each other. "And after everything quietens down, well, then we gather to talk and tell our stories and help each other."

"In this land," she said with no note of arrogance, she simply was stating a fact, "we know how to nail our lives together again. There's a name for folk like us. Rusticators they call us."

She excused herself to go and wait on some men who had come in.

So even the Old Man needs anchoring!

October 1

𝒜 COUPLE OF DAYS AGO in New Hampshire, as we stood gazing up at the stone formation known as the Old Man of Franconia in the Franconia Notch, we saw people busy trying to anchor it so it doesn't tumble.

"Winds 213 miles an hour lash away up there," a native onlooker said. "Remember when you see the Old Man today you'll never see him looking the same again."

Change, I thought. Change attacks solid rocks. Change seems inevitable, an integral part of life. Why then do I resist it?

Today we are in Vermont, and here autumn has struck its match setting the aspens, the maples, and the oak ablaze in flames of red, russet, and burnished gold. Mustard-colored ferns that spread a carpet on the forest floor enhance the trees' foliage. Little brooks frolic everywhere; water tumbles over miniature waterfall after waterfall. The pristine glory of the hills and valleys overwhelms me. Tonight I feel almost drunk with beauty.

Strange but intriguing, I thought as I lay on my bed here in our motel room and reviewed the day, that just before the leaves loosen their hold from the branches and fall to the ground, they glow most brilliantly. I recalled the event on the mount when Christ's face and figure were changed, when his clothes became "dazzling white," causing the disciples to draw back in wonder and alarm. I remind myself this occurred only shortly before his crucifixion. During the ugly days that followed, as evil moved in to destroy their beloved Master, did the disciples recall that glowing event? What meaning did it carry for them?

What meaning can I carry back with me as day after day I now view the leaves, painted crimson and brazen before they will slowly drift to the earth? When my time comes to unclasp my grip and let go of my hold on earthly things and finally life itself, will I be able to do so letting Christ's glory shine through me more brilliantly than it ever did in my "green" years? If that is going to happen, I'm going to have to permit God to bring about some changes in me.

In Hardwood Groves

The same leaves over and over again!
They fall from giving shade above,
To make one texture of faded brown
And fit the earth like a leather glove.

Before the leaves can mount again
To fill the trees with another shade,
They must go down past things coming up.
They must go down into the dark decayed.

They must *be pierced by flowers and put*
Beneath the feet of dancing flowers.
However it is in some other world
I know this is the way in ours.
                              —Robert Frost

Then and now.

October 2

TODAY COVERED BRIDGES and narrow two-lane back roads invited us to explore them; and as we did we passed wooded areas, farmlands here and there with a crumbling barn, people dressed in sweats and sweaters, roadside stands selling maple syrup, small restaurants offering homemade soups and breads, apple sauce, apple cider, apple cake, apple pie, and baked apples. Village greens graced small villages. We saw white-steepled churches, some now used for other purposes than worship, and endless art, gift, and ceramic shops.

We visited a town that, according to some of the plaques in the village square, could trace its history back to a pre-Revolutionary War date. We passed ancient cemeteries and stopping in one, read the inscriptions on the tottering, gray, weather-beaten headstones, commenting on how often a husband's headstone would have the headstones of two wives alongside and next to them small markers bearing the names of babies and young children. I wondered how many mothers had died in childbirth.

"Life is better for us in many ways, isn't it?" we said, holding each other's hands. "We're healthier and living longer, and our infant mortality has dropped way down."

However, we remarked as we continued on our way, perhaps years ago people did better connecting with generations of the past than we do, especially some of us who have moved from the places of our childhood. During these past days we have talked with families who either are living on the same farms their grandparents did or carrying on the same businesses.

This afternoon, looking for a place to stay tonight, a sign outside an ordinary-looking house in a small town caught our eye. It read: "Nothing fancy, just comfortable beds, comfortable prices." We inquired. "Yes," said the owners, a stolid-looking elderly couple. They had room for us.

After settling in, we walked to a nearby café for a bowl of cream of rice soup. When we returned, our hosts invited us to join them in their modest sitting room. As the sign had said, this is no "prettied-up" bed and breakfast house, but just a home opened. The carpet is an out-dated gold, the furniture lived-in and molded to the shapes of people.

They told us that both of them, born and raised in England, were children of doctors. The woman said her mother, who was French, moved back to France after her father died. However, she remained in England; and after France fell during World War II, she couldn't go to France, so she stayed on in London. She had driven an ambulance during the war; London was bombed fifty-five continuous days with incendiary bombs which started to fall about 5 P.M. and continued falling to sun-up. She had driven the ambulance at night in blackout, drove three nights in the week, was on call two nights, and had two nights off. She was young, she said, only twenty-six.

"Mothers were the real heroines," she continued. "The American mothers suffered as they sent the most precious thing they had to a land they knew not, to fight a war that was only indirectly and from a distance threatening to them. The European mothers who knew what it was to have not only their sons' but their own lives endangered, suffered in another way. War is awful!"

Her husband interrupted to say the resourcefulness, initiative, perseverance, endurance, and determination that emerged out of the bombed-out debris and rubble of the bombings was magnificent to see. She agreed but repeated, "War is senseless. It never seems to end; someone is fighting someplace all the time."

Her husband, however, refused to regard things gloomily, reminding her that we are not engaged in a world war now, that they, the two of them, were enjoying life, and that their children were practicing their chosen professions.

"We worked hard to give them their educations," she said. "I stayed home to raise them, but I also took courses in arranging dried flowers, and learned how to apply gold-leaf designs to furniture. And now," she concluded, "now we continue to work so we can earn money to visit them, scattered all over the U.S. as they are, so far away from us."

Home-style cooking—for us.
October 3
Noon, in a restaurant, waiting to be served

THIS MORNING AT THE B-AND-B our hostess spread the breakfast table with old linens carefully ironed. The menu was uniquely hers: apples from their garden cooked with plums, cherry red and tart, they were. Tea made in a *warmed pot*, milk toast with poached eggs and a white sauce that sent floods of memories of winter days at home coursing back when Mother would put a huge bowl of milk toast on the breakfast table.

She carries on, I think. Even when she is tempted to feel discouraged and disillusioned about the way we humans have sometimes messed up the way we live here on earth, still she carries on. A rusticator. And unpretentious and genuine she is, and that I appreciate.

We are drawing close to the end of our New England trip. We have wanted to take some maple syrup home with us so today when we saw a sign advertising maple syrup for sale, we drove up a side road to a house with another building next to it.

As we stepped out of the car a man perched on a twelve-foot ladder, who was painting their house a clear bright yellow, called down asking if he could help us. His wife, on another ladder, was wielding her brush under the eaves.

He invited us inside his shop displaying maple products of every kind. After we had chatted a while he asked if we ever had seen how they process the maple syrup. We told him not now; back in Minnesota years ago some of our neighbors tapped maple trees, built bonfires and hanging huge iron vats over the fire boiled the sap until it was the right consistency.

He then invited us into his plant and explained the process he uses. Finally, turning to us he asked, "And what have you folks done with your lives?"

We told him. He eyed us carefully, then asked what we are doing now. We told him we're retired. He looked steadily at us with his clear blue eyes.

"You're still strong and well. Doesn't your church have anything for you to do now?"

His question haunts me. What am I doing with my life now? Was God asking me the question?

Now the silence, Now the peace,
Now the empty hands uplifted.
—*Jaroslav Vajda*

October 5

THIS AFTERNOON DRIVING ALONG we saw a sign: "WESTON PRIORY. EVENING VESPERS ON FRIDAY, 5 P.M." We looked at our watches. Quarter to five. Should we stop? Why not?
We drove up the road and found the small chapel surrounded by well-groomed and attractively landscaped grounds. We walked into the chapel and sat down. We were the only ones present.

A painting captured my attention almost immediately. Stark in its simplicity it was, a human figure sitting cross-legged, the torso bent over, the arms clasping a huge world globe, the head resting on the globe, expressing powerfully one of my images of God, a God loving the world, claiming the world as his own by his embrace, a God grieving in sorrow for a world torn and ripped apart by animosity, pride, and greed, a God, a risen God who has overcome, but who also remains a bowed-down, burdened God, exhibiting often more sorrow than triumph. And I thought of how some Eastern religions portray Jesus limping through Palestine.

The painting had so powerfully gripped me that I only dimly noticed when a door in front opened and a tall monk garbed in loosely fitting, long, gray flowing robes emerged. Only when he paused beside us did I feel his presence. He inquired if we had come for prayers. We nodded. He told us to follow him and led the way outside and to a gray, weathered barn. As he slid open the door, it creaked. Stepping inside, we were greeted by a rush of warm, moist air, and then I saw that the people crowded inside the barn had produced that warmth. Old, young, whole families, dressed in their work clothes, were seated on wooden benches on three sides of the barn. In front was a semi-circle of chairs. Seeing us standing there some people squeezed together to make room for us.

It was so quiet. No one was saying anything. The old barn door creaked again and again as one by one monks filed in until they had filled the semi-circle. Still the silence. Finally one of the monks, strumming his guitar and singing, broke the silence:

Life is a journey we travel together,
walking hand in hand with our sisters and brothers.

The other monks in the semi-circle and some in the congregation joined in while the rest began to hum along softly. Gentle strumming of the guitar, then another monk began to sing:

A place to go where I can be in silence
and give my heart to you with tenderness.

The words echoed and reechoed in my heart. The song ended. Silence. A long silence, Then the guitar again, a voice singing:

The night is cold and I am cold and lonely;
the day's fatigue brings weariness along.

I missed the next few words, then I picked up:

Come, follow me!
And I go on, thinking there's a meadow
where truth and joy forever dance and sing.

"But where?" I was asking in my heart. Where on this scarred, wounded, broken earth can I find a "meadow where truth and joy dance and sing"? Silence settled within the ancient barn again. No answer to my question? Then the guitar and the voices singing, as though in answer to my unspoken question:

For us to live is to believe

The voices vibrated with joy:

In Jesus, the Christ and in the One who sent him.
... Nothing can take from us that hope
in which we've grown ...

I shut my eyes and let the words settle deep within to marinate until I too began to know silence and quietness in the innermost recesses of my soul.

Reading of scripture, silence, and an opportunity for each to share what, if anything, they had gleaned from the text followed. And then one of the older brothers rose and brought a communion chalice and a loaf of bread to the front. The words of institution were spoken. The loaf broken. The invitation given.

"Let us tear down the walls that divide us," the brothers sang. Two lines formed. My eyes widened as I saw the brothers were offering us, not only the bread, but the wine also. They were tearing down the dividing walls. Tears blurred my vision.

The benediction. One by one the brothers filed out in silence. We followed, also in silence.

"I feel as though I've been on the mount of transfiguration," I said to Luverne as we drove away in our car, "as though I have heard a Voice from above speaking to me too:

> *. . . there was silence in heaven*
> *about the space of half an hour.*
> *(Revelation 8:1)*

> *Harps still,*
> *zithers and psalteries hushed,*
> *cymbals folded, and the note*
> *of alleluias lost*
> *on the farthest height—*
> *only the gentle brushing of their wings*
> *fanning the endless blue,*
> *only the whispered breath*
> *of myriads unnumbered.*

> *Silence while we wait*
> *as the flow of time goes by,*
> *sweet, unhurried, timeless—*
> *while the clouds change shape,*
> *and sunlight, emanating from no sun,*
> *floods all eternity with radiance.*

Silence in heaven,
the vast relief of silence;
while our ears,
filled with too rich harmonies,
hear only the deep
and measured beating
of God's heart.
                    —Mary Esther Burgoyne

The honey gathered. Now sort and store.
October 7

WE'RE ON THE PLANE NOW flying westward home. Fellow passengers are dozing, watching TV, chatting, reading, or working on laptop computers.

I have spent some time leaning back and letting our days pass in review. What have I seen, heard? Have I not heard people quietly and dispassionately talking about how things have changed and were continuing to change? About virgin forests that had been destroyed. About the need (?) to build weapons of destruction in order to provide employment for people?(!) About farmlands disappearing. About today's mobility trend separating older parents from adult children.

But in the midst of the grieving so quietly, expressed or not expressed, had I not seen people with patient courage carrying on? Rusticators. Nailing their lives together again and again.

Had not both people and we commented also how in many ways life today is good: our land is not engaged in a worldwide war; we are a healthier nation, living longer and enjoying medical benefits our parents would have marveled at; more young people are able to attend colleges and pursue careers of their choice; our homes are comfortable; we crisscross the nation in air-conditioned cars on hard-surfaced roads or in planes; and we elders enjoy life in a far richer way than our grandparents and even our parents did.

At the outset of our journey, my concern about the mess our nation is in had so consumed me that it had blocked out in my thinking all the good things life offers me.

Forgetting and ignoring the changes for good which we enjoy, I had set out for a land where I had hoped that maybe change has not taken place, where life has remained as it always has been. How could I have been so naive and innocent, I asked myself, to for one moment think that I could find such a place or to think that if I could find such a land, I would want to return to it? Was it the old in me that had been arguing and fighting to maintain life as I have known it, thinking this would promise me hope and security? Had I been refusing to accept it that change is as necessary a part of life as life and death?

I had begun my journey sick at heart because of all the crime and violence that threaten people everywhere, longing for a time when our grandchildren could play outside and walk the streets in safety, when they could attend schools free of the influence of drugs, alcohol, sexual experimentation, tobacco, and guns. It had been right for me to desire this. But had I recognized that if the poverty that encourages crime is to be alleviated, conflict will result, conflict with mighty corporations fighting for their "right" to employ whomever they wish at whatever wages they wish to work in whatever environment they decide? If the danger that alcohol, tobacco, guns, and pornographic movies and printed material hold for old and young alike is to be dealt fatal blows, won't the companies and cartels behind these fight? *If something new is to emerge, something old must go.* The power of greed, lust, and selfishness must be broken. As pilgrim people we must be prepared to face even more conflict. Appreciation, gratitude, and thanksgiving for all our pilgrims in the community where we live who are working for change wells up within my heart. They have much to teach me.

Our son Dan has been with us this summer also, back from Africa for a couple of months. As I think of him, the peoples all over the world who are poor, hungry, sick, illiterate, homeless, come to mind. What changes will have to come into being in order that life for them will be better? How can these be effected?

I sigh. However, I say to myself, in order to face all the insecurities life inevitably will bring both to me and my loved ones personally, to our nation and the world, I need also a sense of security. I need hope. Where can I find these?

The lines of an old gospel hymn float into my mind:

> *On Christ the solid rock I stand.*
> *All other ground is sinking sand.*

Our trip to New England has rewarded me. My journal contains a quote by Baron F. von Hugel about the lifelong process of producing what he refers to as "The Mature Person." He writes:

> *The great rule is variety up to the verge of dissipation;*
> *recollection up to the verge of emptiness; each alternat-*
> *ing with the other and making a rich fruitful tension.*
> *Thus we gather honey from all sorts of flowers, then*
> *sort out, arrange, unify and store the honey gathered.*
> *After which we again fly out in our honey-gathering*
> *expeditions.*

We have been on a honey-gathering expedition. When we return home we'll begin the task of recalling, sorting out, unifying, and storing the honey. For now I'm going to rest a while. We arose very early this morning to catch this plane. I'll reach up for a pillow, pull down the blind over the window, lean back, and shut my eyes:

A Question of Change

> *"Was there always resistance to change?" I ask.*
> *When first flint lightened tinder,*
> *and pierced round rock became a wheel;*
> *When bark of birch was stretched to frame*
> *and launched upon the tide;*

When arrow shaft was feather-fletched
　　and sapling, sinew-strung, first bent into a bow;
When bird's fine bone became a needle
　　and twisted hair a thread;
When mud was molded, shaped in squares
　　and stacked to form a shelter's wall;
When bogs were drained and dressed
　　and peat first cut as fuel for winter warmth;
When King's divine-right was vanquished
　　and people claimed their power?

"Was there always such resistance?"

The listing could go on and on across
　　the endless years, the eons, and millennia:
　　Papyrus into paper; tin into a horn;
　　Maps to prove the world was round;
　　And instruments to chart the skies,
　　Or peer into a heart;
　　And horseless carriages; Wright Brothers' folly.
　　X-rays, Cat-Scans, MRI's; optic fibre thin;
　　Cell-phones and stereos, T.V.'s interactive;
　　Hubbell scopes, instant film, and micro-chips;
　　Flights in space and walks upon the moon;
Each takes its place in time
　　　　and in the lives of all.

With such evidence before me,
　　of resistance so perverse,
　　Why should I find surprising
　　my heart and will's reluctance—
　　　　the slow-paced change—
　　　　the snail-like metanoia,
　　　　the creeping transformation
　　　　into virtue out of selfishness and vice?
　　　　　　　　—Mary K. Himens

Year Five
and the beginning of Year Six

Learning to Live in Our Ever-New Nows

Ever-deepening gratitude.

December 1

$\mathcal{F}$IVE COMPLETE YEARS have passed since the day the doctor told us tests had revealed a malignant growth in Luverne's prostate. Life has not been the same for us since. To know as a fact that one day life will end is one thing. To have to face head-on that this could happen to me or my loved one much sooner than we had expected is totally different. Luverne is well and strong now; his cancer has not reappeared. Knowing that others have not been as fortunate, we no longer take either life or health for granted but instead begin each day breathing a prayer of humble thanksgiving to God for both these priceless gifts.

We follow with interest reports that now, because of public awareness of the frequency of this disease, the diagnosis is being made in time to have it more successfully treated. Doctors using new procedures to eradicate or palliate it either make recovery easier and less painful with fewer permanent side effects or slow down the progress of the disease.

Joyous anticipation.

January 10

$\mathcal{J}$ANET CALLED TONIGHT, EXCITED.

"Mom, I think I'm pregnant! Wouldn't that be wonderful?"

"How do you know, Janet?"

"I just think I am."

It would be great, wouldn't it, Luverne and I say to each other after we've hung up. We comment again on the amazing recovery she has made from the Guillain-Barré. We recall one of her doctors at Mayo saying as far as he was concerned it was a miracle.

But the Guillain-Barré had postponed their plans to begin a family. Now two years later they have settled in co-pastoring a yoked parish of four congregations in northern Minnesota. The time seems right to begin a family. I am excited.

Earth-shaking tremors.

January 17

THERE WAS A 6.6 EARTHQUAKE UNDER NORTHRIDGE at 4:30 A.M. For us the phone ringing insistently in the dark. "Mom? Are you all right?" Dave calling. I hear children's excited voices in the background. "We're okay. No lights. No electricity. I'm going to check on the gas now. It was a biggie!"

I rolled out of bed, turned on the TV. Called Becky back.

"Dishes on the floor in the kitchen broken. At least one picture off the wall broken. I've lit candles. Water on the floor in the bathroom; maybe water in the toilet splashed over, maybe pipe is leaking. We turned water off. It really shook. Call my folks. We can't call out."

Seven A.M. A phone call from Jackie, the daughter of one of our nieces.

"Are you all right?" We are touched by her concern.

Called Becky.

"Aftershocks continue. Haven't slept much. Can't with six in the bed and everyone jumping out whenever we roll. We'll go to Whittier later and stay with my folks."

I am anxious. Have they checked the freeways? Many are closed. Orders are to stay home. Last night we were on I-10. Took the Fairfax exit. Today that bridge lies crumpled and collapsed.

9:30 A.M.

TV SHOWS AN ENTIRE MOBILE COURT GONE. Fire from leaking gas exploded and spread so fast residents couldn't save anything. They ran. Flames engulfed even their cars. We saw one couple standing immobile gazing at the scene, the elderly man clasping his wife to his chest, her hair just reaching to his chin. A close-up showed her eyes: pale blue, unflickering, empty, staring, unseeing.

The upper level of an apartment building has collapsed into the lower level. An aged couple, still clad in their pajamas, draped with a quilt, pace back and forth holding hands.

One who studies faults and the shifting of earthquakes comments on TV that the anticipated San Andreas quake probably will be ten times as devastating as the one we've witnessed today. We sit on that fault line. I feel jittery. I long to talk to Judy and Janet, but lines are jammed.

9:30 P.M.

A THOUSAND ARE CAMPING OUT TONIGHT in the Sepulveda Basin. Apartments show cracks. People are afraid. They've brought quilts, blankets, and chairs to parks. The city has brought in portable toilets. People are telling their stories to each other. Curfew has been imposed from dusk to dawn. No postal service in some areas. Many schools closed. Transportation officials are planning alternate routes both for commercial and private vehicles. Barricades on some freeways. On the Pacific Coast some hillside homes have slid. Estimate at least six months will be needed to repair I-10's Fairfax exit, our exit to David's.

Anxiety.
January 18

*L*ONG TALKS WITH JANET. She has been spotting. I tell her maybe she isn't pregnant. It's too early to know for sure.

Will you take the time to know me?
January 30

*A*T LUNCH TODAY one of our pilgrims talked about how he had been called back to a congregation he had served years ago to officiate at a funeral. With only one family survivor, a brother who lived two thousand miles away and who would arrive just before the service began, he could meet with no one. The lady, he knew, had been living alone. The little he could recall about her was that she was very old when he knew her, that she spoke little, dressed simply, and had faded blue eyes that darted everywhere. As he headed off for the church, he wondered what he could say about her. Maybe it wouldn't be necessary to say too much. When one lived to as great an age as she, one probably had outlived all who once knew you, didn't one? Except her brother, of course.

Fifteen minutes before the service, as he pulled into the driveway of the church, all the parked cars startled him and more were turning in. He hurried inside. From the sacristy he could hear the sound of folding chairs being set up. When he stepped out to begin the service, he faced a church packed with people. They sang a hymn. He read scripture. As he led in prayer an idea flashed into his mind. What would happen if he gave others a chance to speak? Surely they had come for a reason.

They had. One by one they arose and spoke. Annie was the one who had opened the center for the homeless. Annie motivated them to bring groceries for the hungry. Annie had agitated for a day-care center. Then, as she grew older, she had settled for bringing meals to old people when she heard they were ill. She drove those who were near-sightless or who had no cars to doctors and dentists. She shopped for them.

"I sat astounded," our pilgrim friend said. "At last I arose. My homily was short; enough already had been said, but I spoke briefly about 'Hidden Treasures.'

"The elder brother's eyes were red-rimmed when he gripped my hand at the reception. 'I never knew my sister,' he confessed. 'Once I left home I never bothered to travel back to visit her or invite her to come and visit me. Thank you for making her live for me. I only wish . . .' and his voice trailed off."

Displacement ahead for a young family.
February 2

THE FRONT STAIRS of Dave's apartment has been damaged so they can use only the back steps. The house has cracked in numerous places; they will need to move eventually.

Struggling to trust.

8:15 P.M. February 8

JANET HAS JUST CALLED. She drove to see her doctor today. The blood test showed the sac is empty but an embryo is there. What is wrong? She had made the trip alone, and she said she cried all the way home, but she is going to try and trust God even though she can't understand why all this is happening.

Oh dear God, please spare Janet the suffering I knew.

Paths that take us into the night.

6:15 A.M., February 10

JANET CALLED saying she is having severe abdominal pain. She called her doctor. He said if it continues, come to the hospital.

TWELVE NOON. Janet just called. She had driven to Fargo. Her doctor examined her, did a blood test, is puzzled, allowed her to return home, but ordered her to rest completely.

Though my heart was heavy with anxiety, we went to dinner as usual. A student studying gerontology at Chaffee College, seated at our table, said preliminary studies her class has made show those who have lived to be more than 100 years old (1) were positive-thinking people; (2) had goals and interests to pursue; (3) knew how to face and live with loss. But who wants to live to be 100?

6:30 P.M. Janet again. Her doctor has called. The blood test showed an embryo is growing. He told her to keep in touch with him.

9:30 P.M. Another call from Janet. Her abdominal pain has continued. She called her doctor around nine. He said he has concluded she is about seven weeks pregnant, but something is wrong, has been consulting with another doctor; they wonder if she has a tubal pregnancy. He asked her to be at the hospital by eight o'clock tomorrow morning. They'll do a D and C and search the scrapings. If they find nothing, they will have to do surgery and search. If she has surgery, she'll be hospitalized three, four days. Janet's afraid. I am too. I know that ectopic pregnancies are extremely dangerous and can cause death.

My heart cries out to be with Janet. Why, O God, after all Ron and she have suffered through is this happening? I know, of course, before I utter the question that questions like this one have no apparent answers, but it helped tonight when, as I continued to read C. S. Lewis's book, *Till We Have Faces*, that I came to the part where Orual said, "I know, Lord, why you utter no answer. You are yourself the answer. Before your face questions die away. What other answer would suffice?"

Needed.
9 A.M., February 11

A CALL FROM RON. Janet has had a D and C. They are waiting for results of the scrapings. I wish I was with her.

9:30 A.M. Another call from Ron. They've just taken Janet in for surgery. Luverne is calling about air flights.

Forever his sweetheart.
February 14, Valentine's Day
En route to Fargo to help Janet

WE BOARDED OUR PLANE at 7:30 A.M., sat on it until 10 when we were asked to deplane. Took off on a noon flight. Then Luverne who, after forty-one years of marriage continues to treat me as his sweetheart, handed me a valentine and a parcel prettily wrapped. Inside was one of Barbara's handcrafted enameled pendants.

We missed our connections in Minneapolis, had a three-hour wait. In a few minutes we'll be landing at Fargo. It's almost 9 P.M. The man across the aisle said temperatures outside are in the thirties below zero. Ice slicks the walks and highways. I long to be with Janet. If only I could kiss away the hurt.

The servant role.
February 22

*W*E BROUGHT JANET HOME a week ago, late in the afternoon. Since then she's been in bed upstairs. The doctor has ordered rest and no stair-climbing, so I've been bringing meals up to her. Because doctor's orders had put her flat on her back for some time before we came, I need to clean the house, do laundry.

Luverne, filling in at church, preached at the Ash Wednesday service; but, walking into the house, slipped on the ice, fell, and broke two ribs. He has known excruciating pain since then; I have to help him get out of bed. Neither of us has had much sleep.

The servant role holds little glamour, and yet it is the role our Savior and Lord calls us to assume. If he could, I can.

The people of the parish have outdone themselves in showing kindness. Cards and gifts of food have poured into the parsonage. Telephone calls come, telling Janet not to be discouraged; next time things will go better. Sometimes I think the folks here would like a baby in this parsonage as much as Janet and Ron would! They haven't had one here for forty years.

10:15 P.M.

Was it a coincidence that my reading for this evening was from Matthew 20:22, 26-28 where Jesus asks his disciples, "Are you able to drink the cup that I am going to drink?" And then he goes on to declare, "Whoever wants to become great among you must be your servant—just as the Son of man did not come to be served, but to serve." Carlo Coretto, in commenting on this text, notes that we find it difficult to see God stooping to wash feet. We aren't used to a God like this.

It's so hard to slow down!
March 15, back home

I AM DOING SOME SOUL SEARCHING. When we went to help Janet three weeks ago I plunged into what I considered my task, working hard each day. By evening I was tired but gained satisfaction from tasks completed. I awakened each morning eager for the next day's assignment which I had drawn up for myself. I cleaned. I scrubbed. I scoured. I sorted and set in order. I laundered and ironed. I baked and cooked. With Janet upstairs and the washer and dryer in the basement, I made innumerable trips every day up and down the stairs. For ten days I carried on thus, secretly priding myself that at 72 I still could work so vigorously.

A prolonged plane ride brought us home, and then our absence from the garden summoned me outside to bend and stoop, to rake and prune, to gather up leaves and more leaves.

Now I sit in my reclining chair paying for all my foolish, fevered, compulsive activity performing some tasks which weren't even necessary. My left knee is swollen, on fire, painful and full of fluid. The doctor suspects a torn cartilage. I may choose to have it cared for surgically or let it heal naturally. I have chosen the latter, but this means staying off my feet for goodness knows how long. Foolish, foolish Millie! Why can't I accept it that I can't do some of the things I used to do? And unearth some humility and common sense?

Put the best construction on others' actions.
March 25

A COMMENT MADE AT THE TABLE this noon when one person remarked that young people today "just don't acknowledge gifts they receive" prompted some thinking tonight.

When one becomes old, it's easy to focus on one's slights by others, intentional or unintentional, and on the ingratitude of others, imagined or actual. When this happens, we become unlovely people; others anticipate time spent with us only with a sigh.

In regard to what we perceive to be the ingratitude of others, particularly when it concerns some service given, gift sent and not acknowledged, or help provided, would we not do well to remember and adopt Albert Schweitzer's philosophy? He said as he looked back over his life and recalled the number of people who had helped him in one way or another he was astonished, humbled, and even shamed. Shamed because he realized how few knew how grateful he was; he had never expressed his gratitude, not because he wasn't grateful, he was; but he simply hadn't voiced his appreciation and sometimes out of shyness. Then he moved on to say he would venture many others probably were like him; and that being the case, we justifiably can face the world, seeing it filled, not with self-centered, ungrateful people but rather peopled with truly grateful and appreciative individuals.

If, in our older years, we embraced this philosophy, would we not engage in considerably less talk about people, and especially "this younger generation" being so ungrateful?

The person you know you are.
March 30

ONE OF THE MIXED BLESSINGS of Pilgrim Place is the many informative, even sometimes entertaining, meetings that can easily distract us. I continue to find it difficult to live a disciplined life here. I need time to be alone, so I do not take on the appearance of others, so I can be at home with myself.

Reflection.
April 3

As I LEARN TO KNOW MYSELF BETTER I marvel at the many-sided aspect of my *self*. For example, I see in myself two forces at work. One self longs for intimacy and closeness; the other self longs for independence.

The necessity to exercise and keep these two aspects in balance continues throughout life. We may change as we age. For example, I have seen some women in their elder years becoming more dependent, surrendering the wheel of the car to their husbands even if formerly they drove. In other cases, some women become more independent and assertive and some men more dependent and tender.

I have even seen it in the Health Services Center where a dear friend appears to crave and appreciate affection more than ever in her life at the same time as she still asserts her independence. She declares she sees no reason why at 90 she can't be served eggs for supper if she wants them; and if she can't coax from the cook in the kitchen a baked potato for which she is longing, she uses her phone and asks a friend to bring her one.

I've been thinking about all the talk tossed around about self-esteem. Self-esteem is not a biblical term, but one that has evolved out of a Western culture that places undue importance on the individual. The biblical basis, as I see it, lies in what Saint Paul expressed in I Corinthians 6:20: "You are not your own; you were bought at a price." We esteem ourselves to be of value and worth because a costly price has been paid so we can reconciled to God, be assured of his forgiveness, and, set free from guilt, experience peace. Jesus loved us enough to die for us. This is the basis, the reason for self-esteem.

Parents in pain.
April 9

𝒜 COUPLE OF PARENTS SHARED TODAY their difficulty in knowing how to deal with the pain they are experiencing because a child has made an unwise choice. They know they need to relinquish their child, that they cannot protect or rescue her, and that they ought not to judge her. They know their child is not theirs but God's. They freely acknowledge they gave their child to God and don't want to take her back, but they struggle.

I've found Lewis Smedes's words helpful. In his book *Guilt and Grace*, Smedes differentiates between owning and possessing. He says we possess things, but we own persons, and defines owning as meaning:

- I tell my child we will always belong to each other;
- we let the world know that this child and I belong to each other, thus showing pride in our child;

◆ we thank God for our children, marveling at their uniqueness and rejoicing that we have them and they have us.

Thank God for ordinary days.
April 15

"WHAT KEEPS YOU BUSY these days?" a friend asked when I talked to her today. We haven't seen each other for months.

"Mostly just doing ordinary things," I said. "Toss in a little writing now and again when I can. Visit family, celebrate birthdays. We'll celebrate grandson Jonathan's today. Joel's was a couple of weeks ago; Dave's the end of the month. In fact," I said laughing, "I'm rather glad for ordinary days considering some of the stressful ones we've lived through." As I spoke I was wishing Marta Berg's little poem about ordinary days close by so I could have read it.

A Grand Opening

I saw the sign as I drove by.
"Grand Opening," it said.
Weeks later I drove by the same place.
Again, the sign, "Grand Opening."
How long can a grand opening last?

Then one day I walked past the store,
and I could see two small words
at the bottom of the sign,
"Every day."

They have a celebration every day.
Why, they celebrate the ordinary day!

The ordinary day
devoid of trauma,
free from shock.

The ordinary day,
with its small cares,
its buffered pain.

The ordinary day,
with its sameness,
its tedium.

But . . .

Ordinary day, let me cherish you,
treasure you, hold you close,
for some day, perhaps,
out of ordeal or pain or sorrow,
anguish or torment,
I will long for you with
the deepest longings of my heart,
and I will want,
more than anything in all the world,
your return.

—Marta Berg

People in procession.
April 16

A FRIEND SENT A BULLETIN from one of the Minneapolis
churches telling about a procession held the previous Sunday east
along 31st Street. As those in the procession walked they sang a lament,
"I need you to listen; I need you to answer," and turned into an alley
where a few weeks earlier the body of a murdered woman had been
found. As they continued on their way they heard people calling out of
their windows, "God bless you!" while others watched from their door-
ways and listened as those walking called out the names of more than
thirty men and women murdered amidst the culture of illegal drugs
and prostitution in the city.

Later, as they met together, those who work to rescue young women and men from violence and despair told of their memories of the victims, of their work to change lives, and of their frustration that despite years of efforts, the physical and sexual abuse and the killing continue. They prayed for the families of the victims and called for a community accountability meeting to plan how as a community they can work for change. Oh, that we had more of this concern made visible in action!

Serving God after retirement.
April 18

SOME NEWLY RETIRED RESIDENTS have entered our community which led Luverne and me to talk about retirement this morning as we walked. Now that we're several years removed from that painful experience, Luverne finds it easier to talk about it.

We talked about how Luverne has been adapting. He has found opportunity to teach a Bible class at our church, and from time to time serves as chaplain at our Health Services Center. He fills in when a pastor is absent from his pulpit. He helps here at P.P. in many different ways. He keeps in touch with his former students who are in Christian service all over the world, and he prays for them, but he still misses them. This has been an irreplaceable loss. We talked about the new friends he is gaining, but we mentioned also that friendships take time to develop.

I've been thinking how helpful it could be if our church would introduce a service for the newly retired person, thanking God for what that person has accomplished during their formal work years. If colleagues are present they could speak about what it has meant to them to have their former coworker by their sides. The person who is retiring also could share his ambivalent feelings as he launches out in a new life.

Then prayer could be offered for the retiring person that she may discover the next call God has awaiting her. The fellowship could tell the person what she has meant and means to them personally, thus shifting the emphasis from one of valuing a person for what one *does* or has done to what one *is*. I see a ceremony such as this offering to the retiring person both a time to grieve and a time to be comforted.

Edward's "Ode to Joy."
April 24

DURING OUR WORSHIP SERVICES at church I have marveled as I have observed Edward, who is almost totally blind, singing the hymns —many relatively unfamiliar to me. I asked him today how he does it. He told me the church secretary calls him and gives him the numbers of the hymns for the next Sunday early in the week. With the help of a magnifying machine he can read the words and thus he memorizes them, singing them day after day.

Completing the circle of gratefulness.
April 27

LAST WEEK WE TOOK EIGHT-YEAR-OLD RACHEL with us when we drove north to visit Judy. Six-year-old Jonathan and four-year-old Joel were left at home, so to help compensate for this I prepared a big basket of fruit which I gave to them when we picked up Rachel.

Upon return, as soon as we stopped in front of their house, the children came running out. Everybody else's attention—except Jonathan's —was focused on the sister who had returned home. Jonathan ran straight to us.

"Thank you, thank you, Grandpa and Grandma, for the basket and all the things in it!" he cried, his little face radiating genuine gratitude.

I held out my arms. He came close. We hugged.

Time to say good-bye to Rachel came.

"After a whole week together we'll miss you, Rachel," I said.

"You'll miss me too!" four-year-old Joel cried, jumping up on my lap and winding his arms around my neck. I smiled. How could I do otherwise?

This evening, recalling our visit, my mind flipped back to David Steindal-Rost's statement in his book *Gratefulness, the Heart of Prayer* wherein, writing about human relationships he had commented that the greatest gift we can give is thanksgiving, and "one who says 'Thank you' to another really says, 'We belong together.'" Then he asked a probing question: "Does our society suffer from so much alienation because we fail to cultivate gratefulness?"

Feeling at home.

June 11

"Do you feel at home now when you come back to Pilgrim Place after having been away?" one of our friends asked.

"It's better now," I answer, but when I am alone I ask myself if I can ever expect to feel at home here or anyplace else. The Children of Israel lived for years in Babylon, Joseph lived in Egypt, Ruth in Bethlehem, Mary, Jesus' mother, in many places. We too have our Babylons, our Egypts, our Bethlehems. I think those of us especially who have moved often and lived in many different places, sometimes adopting other countries and cultures for a time, have felt as though we were continually moving from one Babylon to another. That being the case, why should I not accept vagrant feelings of loneliness that pass through me as normal?

But no matter where we have lived I have tried to make a home for our family, planted gardens, worked, given birth to or raised a family, prayed for those among whom I lived, called that place "home." But calling a place home does not mean all loneliness disappears. And in these my latter years should I be troubled if from time to time I do not feel at home? After all, "this world, this world is not my home; I'm just a'passin' through."

Five years ago when I wrote with sadness that I viewed Pilgrim Place as the end of the line, a place where the train went no farther, I erred. Pilgrim Place probably will be the end of the journey for this aging, decaying body, but that will mark but the beginning of the journey God intended for us to make when he created us. When the last breath ceases or gasps its way out of this body, it only will mean getting off one train and boarding another, or to use a present-day figure of speech, an exchange of planes. I don't really want to change planes yet; the flight I'm on pleases me.

My hesitancy in this respect sometimes troubles me, but I know I am not alone in feeling this way. I read the other day about an elderly woman, still living independently, who said every decade has called her to adjust in yet another way. She said she knew the biggest adjustment lay ahead for her: willingness to die; and she found herself struggling and resisting having to accept this. And this woman was 100!

But I am praying God will enable me to look forward more and more to my homegoing, when I shall know him more fully.

Earth people know pain.
June 11

*A*T A GATHERING TODAY reunion with old friends proved to be a pain-filled exposure to the darker, grimmer side of life that we often try to conceal behind forced smiles.

One husband wheeled in his wife. After two back surgeries, she has received no relief for her pain, no freedom from her immobility. One couple was not present, and a friend told us the man lies unable to speak; his wife recognizes no one. Another, who has suffered from chronic pain for years, is receiving treatment now for addiction to pain-killing drugs.

A widowed mother collapsed in tears as she told how she lives in fear of her son, an alcoholic and drug addict. When he appears outside she always locks the door; she talks to him through a closed door. If he wants to talk further with her, she arranges to meet him in a populated restaurant and then, calling a male friend, she asks him to accompany her. A happier note was sounded when a father told of how his son made a trip to Haiti, was so moved by the poverty he saw, he vowed to become a doctor. He has almost completed his training and is seeking direction as to where and how he should serve.

I have found myself reluctant to record the hurt of my friends, but I need to do so to prompt and urge me to lift them in prayer. Nor will I abandon my search for hope. Hope, I read the other day, among other things means being still, waiting for *God*, not waiting for a situation to improve, for that waiting will only interrupt our stillness. I learned this the weeks we lived through Luverne's encounter with cancer and again as we were waiting for the house to sell.

"Pure hope expects the surprise that even the worst, if it happens will be the best," I have noted in my journal, crediting the quote to Brother Steindl-Rost. Talk about that calling for a leap of faith! But one of the reasons we dare to believe this is, as Steindl-Rost assures us, that as soon as the storm is over we "will be growing a new crop of hope."

I don't think we even have to wait for the storm to subside. When we faced Luverne's surgery, I found my new crop of strength and hope growing every night as I slept, ready for me the next morning even though we still were rolling with the storm.

Joy mingled with anxiety.
July 15

JANET HAS JUST CALLED to tell us a test has verified that she is "with child." Joy, joy, joy! But, she says in her next breath, her count is double the usual. Does this mean a multiple pregnancy? I am concerned. Watch over her and the new life within her, Jesus.

More news. Daniel will come to the U.S. in September, spend a year in study, and then hopes to return to East Africa.

God will be with us!
July 31

RON HAS JUST CALLED. Nine o'clock this morning Janet began to have contractions and spotting. The doctor ordered her to come to the hospital immediately. A church member took her. A preliminary scan showed a second fetus in the same tube as before. To save the other baby they did surgery, removing the tube with the fetus. Administering a general anesthesia is not advisable during pregnancy but in this case unavoidable.

I hung up the phone. First I cried. Couldn't help it. Then I called Becky and Judy and my praying friends. Oh, God, dear God! Another loss! Another little one gone. Will the remaining one be unaffected, was unharmed? Please, God.

Can misfortune turn into grace?
8:00 A.M., August 2

A telephone call from Janet at 6:30 A.M yesterday. The doctor will do another scan today. When she finally is allowed to go home, she will have to stay in bed four weeks at least.

This morning I awakened at 4 A.M. Laid and prayed for Janet. Finally slept again. Troubled dreams.

Carlo Coretto wrote that when a mistaken injection paralyzed his leg, it "was not a stroke of bad luck, but it was a grace." Then he clarified his statement saying he would admit it was bad luck, but "God turned it into a grace; it thrust him into new paths." Isn't it true that usually only after one has accepted what has happened, moved into and through the pain, and allowed oneself to be changed that one can make a statement like that?

The need to anchor again.
10:15 P.M., September 3

*J*ANET HAS JUST CALLED. The spotting is continuing. An ultrasound showed the baby is okay, but the area around the surgery has not healed. The baby's movement irritates it, causing bleeding. The wound must heal or she could hemorrhage or miscarry.

Listening to her, the anxiety, the pain, even the terror that twisted and tortured me during my precarious pregnancies arose from my depths within, ascended, peaked, and rushed over me. When I came to the surface, I was sputtering. Wasn't it enough that I went through those experiences? I stormed. Why does Janet too have to walk the same path? Oh, if only I could lay my hand on the wound, touch and heal her! I want to be with her. But when I mention this she says she is concerned my knee hasn't healed enough yet, reminds me they don't have a bed downstairs.

I know she's right. This troublesome, restrictive, limitative hunk of life called aging! *Phooey on it!*

Learning to celebrate in the midst of anxiety.

September 5

THIS MORNING I FROSTED THE CAKE Luverne had baked last night for Ruthie's first birthday party. After lunch we drove to Becky and Dave's home. Eight-year-old Rachel, who had planned the party, had asked us to wear costumes from another country. I wore an African kanga, Luverne wore a shirt made of kitenge cloth. We had fashioned paper flags of Tanzania to wave in the parade that Rachel led, through the house, down the stairs, and outside to the yard to march round and round there. Then we old folks sat on lawn chairs and watched the kids play games. Little Ruthie took a *long* nap and then bewildered, wandered among the guests.

Finally, one by one the guests said good-bye, leaving the grandpas and grandmas with the family. We sat among the debris of scattered toys and paper and ribbons from opened gifts and just enjoyed being together, belonging to each other, encircled and knit together by love. What a gloriously lighthearted, zestful, merry afternoon we had enjoyed! It was so wonderful! We *need* to be with children and young adults, to laugh and play. Sweet, sweet relief.

"Bind us together, Lord, bind us together."

September 14

DAN ARRIVED BACK IN THE U.S., spent a couple of weeks here. He's in Chicago now for study.

"If you want your children to open up to you, open up to them." Someone, can't remember who, once said this. Luverne and I often comment on how thankful we are that our children pour out problems, anxieties, hurts, and joys to us, asking us for our prayers. And the last time one of them called about a concern, this child of ours ended with, "It means so much to have a family like I do to whom I always can turn." Remarks like that both humble and reward me.

We're glad too that they sometimes call each other about concerns they don't wish to discuss with us. That's fine with us.

Oh God, may no misunderstandings, hurt feelings or unforgiving spirits ever sever the invisible bond that unites them. Do I dare hope for this, God? Or is this being unrealistic? Even in your Book we do not read about unscarred families. But if from time to time a wound is inflicted, heal it, oh, Jesus, heal it. After we are gone our children will need each other.

Cheers!
September 29

WE HAD LUNCH TODAY with a 92-year-old, a 93-year-old, and a 94-year-old who kept us laughing throughout our entire meal. In a few days we'll bid good-bye to our friend who celebrated her eightieth with a wow! and whoops! and a yippee! week rafting trip on the Salmon River and soon will fly off to Romania to teach for a short time. Sunday I visited one in her nineties whose blood pressure dropped so low a few days ago it alarmed both the nurses and her doctor. But Sunday I heard her over the phone patiently and sympathetically listening as a troubled, lonely person spilled out her concerns. Finally I heard her say, "Oh, no serious complaints for me. Don't ever worry about me. I'm fine."

"How high was your blood pressure today?" I asked after she hung up.

She shrugged. "Something like 92 over 60," she said. "Makes me feel like an empty sack." Yet no hint of feeling this way had she given to her friend. If I can age like these courageous saints, I'll be happy.

A moment of grace.
October 24

WHEN I TALKED WITH JANET tonight she told how upset she had become because notice about a conference on Christian education had not reached her so she could have sent representatives.

"I was stewing," she said, "when Ron came home. He listened for a while, then walked into the living room and brought a plaque a friend had given me. He handed it to me, pointing at the words as he read them, 'Janet, God danced the day you were born.' I stared at the words and at Ron and felt my irritation being drained away. It was a moment of pure grace, Mom."

Justifiable rage.
December 26, day after Christmas

DAN AND WE ARE HERE celebrating Christmas with Judy's family. We enjoyed our usual round of parties and entertaining before we left, and Dave's family came on the 22nd to be with us.

Today was misty and chilly. Judy had to go to work at the hospital. The children played with their toys, the men alternately conversed or watched the play-offs. I found a quiet corner and began to read a Christmas gift book by Alice Walker and Pratibha Parnar, *Warrior Marks: Female Genital Mutilation and the Sexual Blinding of Women.*

I had known some tribes in Africa practiced female circumcision, but I had not known how extensive and cruel the surgical procedure was in some areas. I had thought it was done to deprive the woman of sexual pleasure. I had not known that in some cases the vaginal opening was crudely and primitively sewn closed to be opened the night of the marriage in order to guarantee the groom that his wife was a virgin. I had not known that if the husband later was absent on a journey, he could, if he chose to do so, have his wife sewn up again to be re-opened upon his return.

I had known mothers and grandmothers participated in the event; I had not thought about the psychological impact when the mother first brings her daughter for the surgery, assuring her it won't hurt, and then holds her down while the grandmothers perform the procedure.

The details given of the surgical procedure in some instances were so horrific I wish I could forget them.

Reading the book, I raged. I fumed. I stormed. I exploded. I accosted Dan. Was this still being practiced? I could not sleep. As I watched the hours on the illumined clock by our bed mark off the hours, I castigated myself. What kind of a naive, innocent person had I been when I had lived in Africa? I had asked no questions.

The hands of the timepiece beside me had arrived at 3 A.M. I'm a different person now, I said, as I shifted restlessly in bed. I've changed. I'm better informed. More aware. Stronger.

What had made me stronger? I asked myself. Was it not the growing solidarity of women giving women courage to ask hard questions, to take risks, to challenge authority, to act together?

If I could return to Africa today to live and work in an area where this brutal, barbaric custom is being practiced, would I remain quiet? How does one differentiate between customs and cultures of others that one needs to reverently respect and practices that are demeaning, inhumane, intolerant, and disrespectful of the value of a woman being equal to that of a man?

What time it was when I finally slept I know not and then it was only to have nightmares torture me and to be awakened at 6:00 when an earthquake rattled the house.

Undying love.
December 29

A BASKETFUL OF CHRISTMAS CARDS and letters greeted our return. Those from our peers, while articulating faith, hope, and joy, struck a somber note also. Pronounced also was the reference to and emphasis on family. Gone are the accounts of work and career—faded into the background.

How true this is for Rex, I thought this afternoon as I was visiting someone in the Health Services Center. Jessie still lives on, but is failing fast now. She no longer can hold up her head. I see little response from her even to Rex; but yesterday as I walked in the doorway, I saw Rex kneeling before her.

"Jessie," he was saying softly, "do you want a kiss?"

To my amazement she raised her bent head and puckered.

I was in the garden room at the Center today arranging some flowers for an occupant when Rex walked by the door. Seeing me, he stopped, and reaching in his pocket handed me a piece of paper. I wiped off my hands, unfolded the paper, and read it.

My Love

My love for you is destroying my heart.
   The flame that was you
     is flickering, dying.
It lit my path.
   I stumble as the lights grow dimmer.
My life has been a pilgrimage,
   your heart the grail.
   I followed the gleam
     joyfully, passionately.
But now darkness.
   Where now do I go? How now do I see?
My love for you is destroying my heart
   yet it is the most precious thing I possess.

I stood staring at my flowers. Rex had disappeared down the hall. Just as well. What would I have said?

But how mysterious love is, I thought. Not dependent on physical attractiveness. Not even on the ability to respond. Or talk. Or smile. Or carry one's share of the load. Love, true love, never fails. And not only does it not fail, but paradoxically, in the very difficulty of continuing to love generously, it finds joy, a joy riddled with pain, but joy.

Difficulty in continuing to love? Maybe I erred in using the word "difficulty." If we love passionately, as Rex describes his love, continuing to love—regardless—is not difficult. Demanding? Yes. Painful? Yes, because love brings joy but also sorrow. You cannot have one without the other. That is the price of loving, the price of knowing joy. But difficult in the sense of finding the will to continue to love? No. And thus through the loving and the grieving and the suffering the souls can expand and grow so when the call comes, those called can accept and bear their cross with courage and dignity, again and again moving into new nows, thus fulfilling more completely the role God created them to fill.

I see how in another sense also Rex's life has expanded and grown. Up until the time Jessie became ill, his calling had taken him into the realm of outward activity with all that had involved: planning, administration, and management in addition to pastoral responsibilities. When Jessie became ill, Rex heard and responded to another call, this time a call to develop the nurturing, mothering, caring aspect of his personality; and in responding to that call he discovered, in spite of weariness, an undreamed of potential within him to give and give and give, day after day, a potential women often discover after they have borne children.

A new year of grace.
8:00 P.M., January 5

WE GOT UP AT 4 A.M. Took Dan to the airport. He's back in Chicago continuing his studies.

As we begin this new year we give thanks to God, having rounded the corner and completed six years now without Luverne's cancer reappearing.

Whoops! A call from Ron has just come, raising concern. The doctor has hospitalized Janet. Her blood pressure and weight have soared. She can't get her shoes on, her ring off. Her protein count is low, low, low. Toxemia. The doctor has ordered bed rest for her from now on; they are hoping to "buy six weeks' time." Please, God. I'm afraid.

No place left untouched.

January 8

WE HAD INVITED A 92-YEAR-OLD FRIEND who lives in an apartment unit for seniors in a sleepy Midwestern town to have dinner with us. She told of their 70-year-old caretaker committing suicide, shooting himself outside her door. Why?

Because a resident had accused him of molesting her. Is the story true? No one knows. But now the apartment unit, which used to be one where people left their doors unlocked and neighbors wandered in and out to chat and drink coffee, has become a building of locked doors and frightened neighbors suspicious of each other.

We talk to Janet daily.

Yah, that's the way it is now.

January 9

THESE DAYS WHEN ANXIETY GRIPS ME from time to time as I think about Janet and her baby, I thank God for every bit of comic relief I receive. A table companion at noon today brought a smile to all of us when he said, "One way I know I'm getting old is because when I'm about to bend to tie my shoes I ask myself first if there is anything else I want to do while I'm stooped down."

That prompted me to tell them about what had happened to me a few nights earlier. My body prodded me to go the bathroom. I rolled out of bed and still in a stupor of sleep wove into the bathroom where I had forgotten to turn on the night-light.

"I sat down," I said, "but instead of sitting down where I should, I landed in the bathtub with my legs hanging over the rim. That woke me up. I swung my legs into the tub and was contemplating how I could get out—we haven't installed grab bars yet—when the lights went on, and Luverne stood in the doorway.

"'Whatever are you doing there?' he asked.

"'Just taking a bath, Dear,' I said."

Before you speak, walk in another's shoes.
January 11

YESTERDAY AND TODAY I've felt I was living in timelessness. Visual images of the starkly simple room in the seven-bed hospital in Africa where I spent two months at the time of Janet's birth push themselves to the forefront of my mind's eye. Her call this morning almost caused me to panic. Her blood pressure and fluid retention are not under control. The doctor hears the movements of the uterus contracting.

Janet was sobbing. "I'm afraid," she said. "I'm afraid."—the two words she cried out to me again and again when the Guillain-Barré paralyzed her.

I called someone I thought would understand and pray.

"You said she's only in her thirty-first week?" she asked. "Oh, well, I wouldn't be concerned. Maybe it's better if it ends. Something might be wrong."

I felt my mouth gape open.

"I think I hear someone at the door," I lied. "I have to go," and I hung up. For a brief moment I hated her. Then one of our African proverbs rose out of the depths of my stored memory, rescuing me: "He who makes light of a wound knows no scar." But it isn't only Janet who is afraid. I'm afraid too. Save us, Lord!

The critical situation worsens.
January 21

WE TALK TO JANET DAILY. Things have quietened down a little.

"But be on call, Mom," she says.

Dave and Becky will move next Saturday. We'll bring meals and take the three oldest children home with us while Becky and Dave unpack and settle in.

One goes; one stays.
February 15

LUVERNE FLEW BACK ON FRIDAY to help Janet and Ron. Monday it rained, and I enjoyed taking a walk in the rain. Guests have visited. Dan called Valentine's Day to tell me he loves me; Judy and all the grandkids called too.

Living alone I've discovered how many lights *I* leave on; I had thought Luverne was doing this. I've been working in the garden planting some perennials. Brought home impatiens, azaleas, and snapdragons to tuck in the soil. The garden promises to look right pretty.

911 call to me.
8:30 P.M., February 16

WHAT TIME WAS IT the first call came? Around five, I think; I was working in the garden. Janet was concerned about something that was happening. I told her to call her doctor.

Went back to my garden to finish the planting. Was potting the last impatiens when Luverne called. The doctor had told Janet to wait and see what developed.

"I have a very strong feeling that I should get ready to leave," I said.

Went out again. Darkness was creeping up rapidly. Started to dig to put in the azaleas. Hard soil and rocks resisted me. Brought out our big flashlight. Tried to finish digging and lining with peat moss by the light of the flashlight's narrow beam. Difficult. Finished finally. Ate a sandwich at eight. Scanned and sorted day's mail. Too tired to do anything more. Too tired even to pray. Hope God understands. I'll drag myself to bed. I'll tackle the packing tomorrow.

Scrambling.

February 17, airborne for Fargo

A YEAR AGO ON VALENTINE'S DAY Luverne and I had been airborne to care for Janet after her surgery for tubal pregnancy. Now here I am again!

Luverne's first phone call awakened me at midnight.

"Janet's leaving for the hospital."

Janet took the phone. "I've a terrible headache, Mom. Have a bad cold on top of all the other, cough so hard, haven't been able to sleep."

I was so tired that, worried though I was, after we hung up I fell asleep again. At five in the morning the phone shrilled me awake again. Luverne.

"I'm coming, Honey," I said. "I'll try to catch the noon flight. Go standby if I can."

Stayed up. Called a friend who is an early morning riser. Could he take me to the airport? He could if we could leave an hour and a half early. Flew around. So many people to call, so much to think about. Watered newly planted flowers. Set timer for lights. Notified security and dining room of absence. Arranged for mail to be brought in the house. Called Bernice to take over the writing group. Asked Ned to feed the cat. Called Judy and Becky. Thanked Becky again for bringing me some days ago her down coat, mittens, knitted cap, and leggings. Called Nabor about watering. He couldn't understand my English, had to get someone to interpret. Returned library books. Stopped paper. Packed.

The flight so far is fantastic. So clear. Grand Canyon today spectacular. So HUGE. Skimmed over the mountains, saw them snow-covered and in places embroidered with ski trails. Land below us now is flattening out.

I fly with hope, trust, and prayer, carried along knowing many are praying. What a prayed-for baby this one has been.

Dear God, may Janet's pain in giving birth not be too severe. Help her. Ease her anxiety.

I wonder if the child has been born. I'm tempted to use the phone and call. I'm tired, tired. I have a two-hour wait in Minneapolis. Wonder if my dear friend Thyra will be there to meet me.

Unto us a child is born.

February 18

$\mathcal{A}$RRIVED AT FARGO AIRPORT 9 P.M. last night. Luverne was waiting. Got to the hospital around 9:45. Met the doctor in his scrubs in the hallway outside Janet's room.

"She's pushing hard," he said.

"Do you want some coffee?" one of the nurses offered. "Let me show you where the Family Waiting Room is."

As I watched the hands of the wall clock climb toward midnight, the mother feelings within me climbed. I longed to be with my child at this time—especially this time—because this was her first experience of giving birth. I longed to stand by her side, to reassure her, to pat her damp, hot face with a cool cloth, to stroke back gently her hair, to tell her she was doing nobly; I wanted just to be with her. But today's practices have changed all that. Egisto Lancerotto's oil painting of a grandmother with the newborn on her knees as she prepares to swaddle the infant no longer represents life today. Years ago the father sat outside the door, the hut, the tent, smoking and waiting. Nowadays it is the grandmother pacing in the hallway outside the door, waiting, praying, worrying.

And worry I did. I knew Janet had one of the finest doctors one could find coaching her, cheering her on. I knew Ron was by her side. But still I worried.

The waiting room could not restrain me. From time to time the doctor would emerge. When he began to say, "Her pain is so bad," my heart weakened.

Again and again he emerged. "Her pelvic area is small." "She's not dilating as she should." And finally, "I won't wait much longer. If something doesn't happen soon, I'll have to do a C-section. I don't want to. She already has had two major surgeries this year. But I may have no choice."

I felt my wings of faith and trust stiffen with fear. I could no longer mount up; I was belly-flopping. Luverne took my hand. "Let's go to the waiting room and pray," he said.

We did. We uttered few words. I held my head in my hands.

What if the baby doesn't survive? What would this do to Janet?

Oh, no, God, I cried.

Our little parchment prayer that had rescued me during Luverne's cancer encounter had been lost in our moving. No matter. The words remain engraved on my heart. I groped for them. "So give me the strength I need. So give Jana the strength she needs—for whatever." Unuttered prayers. Prayers to breathe.

Midnight, says the wall clock. And then finally at 12:15 a cry. We jump to our feet to meet Ron in the hallway. A little girl! All is well. Thank God!

The nurse carries her out. We watch as she weighs, measures, and swaddles her. She hands her to Ron, who in turn hands her to me. At last. Perfectly formed. Oh, thank you, God! What a cute pug nose. What a treasure!

And finally I can see Janet. I cry. Though she says nothing about it, I can tell instantly how she has suffered.

Arrived at our motel room at 2:00 A.M. We were too excited to sleep. Too full of joy. By 3:00 A.M. we were still awake.

We're back at the hospital now. Will spend most of the day here. Toward evening we'll drive to Ron and Janet's home. Luverne will preach in two of the churches tomorrow. Youth are conducting services in the third church.

In love with a child.
10:35 P.M., February 27

LUVERNE PREACHED IN TWO CHURCHES YESTERDAY. Snow had fallen during the night. I don't have boots; couldn't get to church..

Janet and baby finally came home this afternoon. Because Alisa's bilirubin climbed, she was placed in an isolette to get light treatment. We have been driving back and forth while Janet and she have been in the hospital.

Judy, Becky, and David have called several times. Friends at Pilgrim Place have called too, also my brother and our niece back East who is a doctor. People care.

I love to hold little Alisa. In the hospital the nurses would take her out of the isolette and put her in my arms. Since Janet has come home I haven't wanted to relinquish her. I look and look at her. With sheer delight I bend my head and kiss her soft cheek, and softly sing to her a children's hymn my mother sang to me.

I Am Jesus' Little Lamb

I am Jesus' little lamb,
Therefore glad at heart I am;
Jesus loves me, Jesus knows me,
All that's good and fair He shows me,
Tends me every day the same,
Even calls me by my name.

Should not I be glad all day
In this blessed fold to stay,
By this holy Shepherd tended,
Whose kind arms, when life is ended,
Bear me to the world of light?
Yes, O yes, my lot is bright.
    —*Henriette Louise von Hayn, 1778*

Who am I?
February 28

AIRBORNE AGAIN EN ROUTE HOME. My arms can still feel little Alisa cuddled against me. To have my arms filled again with a new life satisfies my heart so completely. I think I remember something Barbara Ascher wrote about being in love with a child is like being in love with your sweetheart. It colors everything. Joys become more joyous, forgiveness more generous, compassion more compassionate. The sky is bluer, the roses smell sweeter, the moon shines brighter. We really aren't to be trusted when we are in love with a child.

Everything seems more than it is, exaggerated. And who wouldn't have it so?

I see it in my journal entries also. I've been sitting here flipping back the pages and rereading. I can't miss the contrast: the turmoil, the anxiety, the skittering up and down the scales of faith, the weakening of hope, the tremblings, the steadyings, the calmness. In some entries I even have noted finding "green pastures and still waters," of experiencing "rising up with wings like an eagle and soaring, of running and not being weary, of walking and not fainting." Some emotions extreme? Perhaps.

At the same time, the contrast in the entries leaves me puzzled. *Which one am I?* I cry. Dietrich Bonhoeffer uttered that cry during his long months of confinement in a Nazi prison cell as he found himself alternately strong and weak.

"Who am I, God? This one or the other? Am I one person today and another tomorrow? Sometimes one person in the morning and another person in the afternoon? Am I both at once?" I ask myself. I am a puzzle to myself, a contradiction. But one thing I do know. Whatever, whoever I am, I belong to you, Jesus. I am yours.

Absurd Paradox

Joy/Pain
floods/parches
fertile fields/desert spaces
where songs burst/where sighs pierce
dikes of humanness/aches of loneliness
ecstatic stirrings/muted cries
vibrant Life/sacral DEATH

Death/Life
Pain/Joy
O sterile fruitfulness/and fruitful sterility
A loving loss/and losing love
Absurdity in order/and ordered absurdity.
    —Mary K. Himens, SSCM

Song of home.

March 1

*A*ND SO WE'VE COME HOME. This morning, with my body's clock still set at Midwestern time, I awakened early. Luverne continued sleeping. I showered, dressed, and drove to pick up milk and bread. Standing at the checkout counter I felt arms around me.

"Millie! You're home. So glad you're back. How's Janet and the baby?"

It was one of the men from church. As we stood chatting, another man from church came in. A big smile, another bear hug, a warm greeting.

I was getting out of my car here at home when one by one I saw our Cambridge Way family come out their doors to welcome me with hugs. As I stepped in the house the phone was ringing. It hasn't stopped all day. We have felt loved, cared about, secure.

Is it a coincidence that today marks our fifth anniversary of moving into this community? Today from the bottom of my heart I can say, "I have come home." I believe that once again we have negotiated a decisive turning point, one of many, but a major one. Looking back we can note completion of a number of other departures, all of which have helped lead us into this new now.

What remains ahead? Only God knows. But with God and our little parchment prayer we'll make it.

At one of our last vesper services we sang a hymn by Hugh T. Kerr that sums it up for me so well:

> *God of Our Life, through All the Circling Years*
>
> *God of our life, through all the circling years,*
> *We trust in thee;*
> *In all the past, through all our hopes and fears,*
> *Thy face we see.*
> *With each new day, when morning lifts the veil,*
> *We own thy mercies, Lord, which never fail.*

God of the past, our times are in thy hand;
With us abide.
Lead us by faith to hope's true promised land;
Be thou our guide.
With thee to bless, the darkness shines as light,
And faith's fair vision changes into sight.

God of the coming years, through paths unknown
We follow thee;
When we are strong, Lord, leave us not alone;
Our refuge be.
Be thou for us in life our daily bread,
Our heart's true home when all our years have sped.
　　　　　—Hugh T. Kerr, 1872-1950, alt.